PENGUIN BOOKS

BORN AGAIN ON THE MOUNTAIN

Arunima Sinha is the first female amputee (and the first Indian amputee) to climb Mount Everest. She is currently setting up a free sports academy for the poor and differently abled persons.

Manish Chandra Pandey is a Lucknow-based special correspondent with several years' experience in print media.

PRAISE FOR THE BOOK

'One can give a lot of good quotes to others – like "success lies in courage" or "where there is a will there is a way" . . . but these abstract concepts in themselves are not going to inspire. What is courage, what is willpower is brought out by Arunima's story. I had seen this in her when she met me soon after she got out from AIIMS, New Delhi. I asked her, "Will you be able to climb with an artificial leg?" Her commitment to the Everest was total and I found her to be very focused on her goal, after which I started training her. Arunima is one person who, I found, always challenges herself. While others may doubt her abilities, she believes in herself and creates new paths for herself. I am sure the book is going to inspire all those (particularly women) who lack the Can Do spirit and the motivation to take control of their lives'—Bachendri Pal, Chief, Adventure Programmes, Tata Steel

'Arunima's life is one of the bravest of the brave! One in which she went far beyond herself and proved beyond any doubt that where there's a will there's a way. An inspiration to all who are looking for those extra reserves, Arunima's life says, "Never say enough is enough!"' —Kiran Bedi, former IPS officer

'Arunima Sinha's life and struggle is an inspiration for all humanity' —H.R. Gaikwad, Chairman and Managing Director, BVG India Ltd

'If you are looking for a book on crisis management, here it is – the best one. Arunima Sinha's story is at once thrilling and inspiring and is a practical demonstration of the message of Swami Vivekananda – "Faith, faith, faith in ourselves, faith, faith in God – this is the secret of greatness."'—Swami Nikhileshwaranand, Head, Ramakrishna Mission, Vadodara

BORN AGAIN ON THE MOUNTAIN

A Story of Losing Everything and Finding It Back

ARUNIMA SINHA

with Manish Chandra Pandey

PENGUIN BOOKS

An imprint of Penguin Random House

PENGUIN BOOKS

USA | Canada | UK | Ireland | Australia
New Zealand | India | South Africa | China | Singapore

Penguin Books is part of the Penguin Random House group of companies
whose addresses can be found at global.penguinrandomhouse.com

Published by Penguin Random House India Pvt. Ltd
4th Floor, Capital Tower 1, MG Road,
Gurugram 122 002, Haryana, India

First published by Penguin Books India 2014

10 9 8 7 6 5 4

ISBN 9780143423706

Typeset in Sabon by R. Ajith Kumar, New Delhi
Printed at Manipal Technologies Limited, India

www.penguin.co.in

To countless anonymous Indians who have been,
in their own ways, helping the needy. My being alive
is proof that they exist.

To Bachendri Pal and the Tatas – without
your support and encouragement, I would
never have had a chance to scale the Everest and
make a new life for myself.

I WAS LYING BETWEEN TWO RAIL TRACKS.

The night seemed deathly still and I could hear my heart throb wildly. The end appeared to be just another train away. Trains thundered past, eerily close to me. I could hear their angry hisses, smell the stink of the human waste that got thrown from the moving trains near me, and feel the sparks of the wheels against the iron railroad.

Here I was – lying on the gravel-filled track-side space, shivering with cold and fear, clutching two stones tightly to control the excruciating pain. It seemed as if I had been thrashed by a sledgehammer. My body was soaked in my own blood. My left leg had been run over by the train, the right was battered, with numerous broken bones and severely damaged ligaments; both motionless. My vision was blurred due to the blood loss. Every part of my body was in agony and I couldn't stop crying. The pain kept getting worse, until it became far too much to handle.

I fainted.

Things didn't improve when I regained consciousness. If anything, the pain got even worse until finally my body, unable to bear the torment, became numb. Every now and then, the rail tracks would tremble to indicate the thunderous arrival of yet another train. And each time a train ran past me, raising the same cruel shriek, I thought to myself that I wouldn't live to see another one. Those insensitive steel bogies seemed to be mocking my helpless state. Thankfully, unlike my body, my mind was active still.

'Don't let your arms and limbs fall on the tracks . . . control yourself from falling over . . .'

My family, especially my father, a proud army man, had taught me to try till the last. So I tried. '*Bachao . . . bachao* . . . Someone help please . . .' I screamed; less in hope, more to shout the fear away. I doubt if anyone heard me. Continuous blood loss meant my body's energy reserves were depleting fast. Soon my screams had turned to whimpers.

Anyway, who would be there in the dead of night,

in the middle of nowhere to hear – or maybe 'care to hear' – such calls? In this suspicious and selfish age, it requires great strength of character to respond or even to think of responding to calls for help at such an unearthly hour. How would I have responded to calls for help in a similar setting? But this was hardly the time or place for philosophical musings.

My thoughts were interrupted by things moving on my body. I remembered to my horror that rodents don't require an invitation, especially on rail tracks. They were all over me pretty quickly, some of them – perhaps taking me to be dead – began probing me, with the more adventurous ones even attempting to feast on my flesh. I was powerless to stop them, unable to move my hands and legs. They nibbled along, nervously at first and then finding no resistance, the bigger rats started pouncing all over my body, making small, spooky squeaks.

'Hush . . . hush . . .'

I tried to scare them away. But they were hardened creatures. Too busy to take notice of my hollow threats, they scurried all over my body, until the tracks began to tremble again. That was an indication for me and them too, about the arrival of yet another train. I knew the slimy creatures would vanish temporarily only to reappear after the train was gone. Every now and then, tears rolled from my eyes. But even crying felt tiring. I wondered if my tears had left a dirty trail on my cheeks, just as they used to when, as a kid, I got thrashed by my parents for being cheeky. Back then, the thrashing came with rewards, halwa-poori et al . . .

. . . My mind had become a cocktail of emotions.

As the rail tracks trembled again, I shuddered. Would this be my last? I tightened my grip over the stones. A minute later, I let out a sigh of relief. This train too, like the forty-eight before it, had spared me. I was still breathing! Indeed, I thought, there was some power that wanted me to breathe, to fight and to win. I could still feel the gold chain round my neck.

And strangely enough, staring at the stars, I managed a smile.

THEY SAY OUR LIVES ARE SCRIPTED IN ADVANCE.

We just play our part and fate intervenes in mysterious ways to ensure that no one deviates from the script. In my case, it was a wrong date of birth on my Central Industrial Security Force (CISF) interview call letter that led to my taking the train journey that changed the course of my life forever. The call letter from the CISF was very important for me and my family. My family consisted of my mother Gyan Bala, my sister Laxmi, her twelve-year-old son Raja and husband Sahib, and Rahul, my brother.

We desperately needed the job. On my brother-in-law Sahib's (who was with the Central Reserve Police Force [CRPF]) suggestion, I had applied for a head constable's post. I had always been athletic and had previously represented my school in football and later my college at national-level volleyball. And I played a bit of hockey too! Girls weren't encouraged to take up sports, especially in east Uttar Pradesh, where I come from. My name was often proposed when the school authorities required representation for any sporting activity, so much so that many people in Ambedkarnagar, my hometown, started calling me *ghamanja khiladi* – roughly meaning an all-rounder.

Having filled up hundreds of job applications so far without getting any response, I knew that this 'call' was special. It was quickly decided after a brief family gathering – in most poor families who have nothing to lose, family meetings are surprisingly businesslike and decisions are arrived at without much fuss – that ahead of the interview, I needed to make a dash for the CISF Greater Noida office to get the mistake rectified.

On 11 April 2011, my elder sister escorted me to the Charbagh railway station in Lucknow from where I was to board the Delhi-bound Padmawat Express train. She gave me a quick hug and left and I walked alone to the ticket booth. The good thing about travelling in the general class is that even though a seat is not guaranteed, the ticket always is. Invariably one manages to eke out space no matter how choc-a-bloc the compartment might be. If nothing else, one at least gets a door handle to latch on to. I doubt if you have ever seen a general class ticket holder return from the station because of lack of space in the compartment. There is room for everyone.

Our country's employment scenario too is like the general class of a much-in-demand train, with several people vying for every seat. The only difference is that while the general class of a compartment accommodates everyone, the job market leaves several of the poor jobless and dejected. The booking clerk at the general class ticket window was a turbaned Sikh. He asked me for change when I extended the only Rs 1000 currency note I possessed. '*Khulla do* (give change),' he said, a touch of irritation in his voice. Though I sympathized with him, leaving the queue to fetch change would have meant waiting for another thirty minutes.

No one behind me in the queue seemed to have change. I remember asking a couple of people standing behind me but they all conveyed a 'no' with an identical shake of their heads. I didn't believe them. After all everyone carries some money while travelling. But everyone is eager to advance, in a queue or in life. There is nothing wrong with this but the real problem is that usually people prefer to do so at the cost of others.

But I was used to managing on my own. And so I decided to do something that comes naturally to most Indians – argue! I won, after a gruelling seven-minute round, with a ticket to Delhi as the reward of my arguing skills. As I approached the Padmawat Express, I was gripped with nervous excitement. After all, I was just a couple of steps away from the coveted job!

Finding the general class was easy. It was the only largely-male compartment, in which passengers were squashed like sardines. Curious eyes followed me as I entered the compartment holding my mobile phone in one hand, a folder that had my certificates in the other and a backpack stuffed with some essentials.

Despite girls having invaded several so-called male frontiers, they are still seen and even referred to as the 'weaker sex'. Such descriptions of women just strengthen gender stereotypes. A woman might be physically weak, but what about mental strength? Though clearly, mentally far superior – this aspect is rarely highlighted – women are looked upon as 'objects' even today.

That perhaps explained the curiosity which I had generated among the males inside the compartment. I had a vague feeling that a few eyes were staring at me in a rather probing way. Women across the country have learnt to live with these 'looks'. In metros and other urban centres girls are now competing with men. Yet there are people who still believe that most women on top have had to take the 'casting couch' test to get to where they are. Of course, this is absurd. But the belief that males advance on merit, while women depend more on their sexuality remains popular in small towns and villages. Even in big cities, the thinking continues to be small. Irrespective of the setting – rural or urban – women are constantly subjected to scrutiny; their actions and reactions endlessly dissected, debated and discussed. Have you ever heard of a male taking an *agni pariksha* or a character test? Invariably it's women. We hear so much about rape these days – I have no doubt that the rapists are not doing this for pleasure but to establish their control over women.

Anyway, why was I thinking all this? The more important thing was to grab a corner and settle down. I looked around to see if there was any space to sit. There seemed none at the moment even though I knew that by the time the train moved there would be space for everyone. Right now it required an effort to even stand without being pushed around inside the compartment. I could see people sitting on the floor, inside the toilet, some sharing the toilet seat too. On a solitary seat near the window at one corner sat a youth who must have come early to be in such an advantageous position in this 'cattle class' compartment. I sensed that the young man was 'human enough' and may yield space to a girl. Reluctantly, I approached him with a 'seat sharing' offer. Much to my relief, he agreed.

I thanked him for his generosity but felt a twinge of guilt at having got the man to share a seat which he must have secured after braving many blows and painful nudges. We adjusted on the same seat. It was around 11 p.m. when the train, that had been slightly delayed, began to move. Finally, I was on my way to Greater Noida where I knew that the first task was to get the date of birth corrected. Once that was done, I had to concentrate on my interview. And thereafter I hoped to bag the coveted job!

I had started dozing off. After a while the whole compartment went silent. Everyone wanted to catch some sleep before the next station arrived. I tried to remain alert and awake, given the fact that I was sharing a seat with a young man. The train had gathered speed by now, though every now and then it slowed down or even stopped for a while. The doors of the compartment were open on my side; apparently to provide additional space to those sitting at the entrance or to accommodate late entrants who latch on to the door handle, keeping half their body inside, the other half outside, in a perfect but illegal and highly dangerous balancing act.

A couple of hours quickly slipped past in this manner. Even with my eyes closed I could sense when the train slowed down, or stopped and people either stepped out of my compartment or moved in. I remember someone saying that Bareilly railway station would come after some time. My eyes were closed, but my mind was awake. In fact I was engaged in silent, mental soliloquy. 'Delhi isn't far from Bareilly. Once there, I will go straight to the CISF office in Greater Noida . . . I wonder what the CISF people will ask me . . . But I will handle the queries. My case is strong enough. The error happened at their end . . . I had mentioned the correct date of birth while filling up the form. They made a mistake . . .'

I was deep in thought when I felt a hand tugging at my gold chain. A girl's sixth sense is always her best companion. In fact even before I actually felt the hand, I had this uncanny feeling that something sinister was about to unfold. Jolted from my reverie I instinctively opened my eyes to see four or five young men around me. Their drunken looks and wayward behaviour gave me an inkling of their background and intention. They were looking for easy prey in the general compartment.

Naturally, a lone girl fit their description of easy prey perfectly. The manner in which they eyed my gold necklace had me in no doubt that they were rather eager to strike gold quickly. I stood up in a flash to tell them that I had no intentions of parting with my chain. It was my mom's gift to me, a precious gift. So they came at me together.

Even though the compartment was full, none of my fellow passengers got up to even inquire what was happening – forget about coming to my rescue. This is another big problem in the country. We rarely speak up for others, thinking it's 'their' problem. Of course when it is our problem, we expect the world to help. The louts targeted some others in my compartment as well. But even they kept silent.

As kids, I often fought with my younger brother. That had something to do with our upbringing. I was brought up like a son, subjected to the same tasks, exercises and, of course, the same punishment that my brothers used to get. If ever I needed to fall back on that courage, resolve and training, it was now.

From the way the wolves came at me, it was clear that they weren't mere pull-and-run chain snatchers. They were hardened criminals, who wouldn't think twice before attacking a girl. I had no option but to take them on. So I caught a youth, who was trying to size me up, by his collar and remember pushing him back. I kicked a couple of others. An unusual battle had begun inside a train on the move. Since I was young, physically fit and an athlete, I was able to hold them off longer than others. As another guy pulled me from behind in an obvious attempt to unsettle me, I swivelled around and hit him. Furious and taken aback at the unexpected resistance I had offered so far, he came back at me with renewed force.

I was still grappling with him, when his other mates also recovered and took me on. The wolves made another attempt to snatch my chain. I remember kicking a couple of them but they were far too many for any lone girl to handle. I had already held them off longer than expected. But to be fair, even the louts had persisted for a period longer than I expected them to. Someone had to give in now.

Frustrated and apparently embarrassed at not being able to prevail over a lone girl, the vandals got nasty. One of them kicked my stomach, forcing me to double up in pain. As I cowered under the impact and held on to the door handle for support, yet another youth kicked me. My grip loosened on the handle.

I was trying to regain balance, when I was hit again. The sight of me floundering had probably given the wolves in human garb a kick. Their confidence restored, the ruffians came at me again and again. Still, I resisted – until one of them, driven by a mad frenzy, gave me an extra hard kick, using all his force. Off balance, I couldn't recover in time.

I literally flew out of the train, still holding my mobile phone though the folder containing my certificates had already fallen somewhere by now. I was mid-air when fate scripted a cruel tale. I flew right into another train that happened to be moving on the next track. My body hit moving steel and lobbed automatically in the air towards the other train – on which, seconds ago, I was travelling – on the rebound.

The ping-pong must have continued for several

seconds before gravitational force pulled me down. I thud-landed perilously close to the railway track. Despite my efforts, my left leg fell on the track over which one of the trains was still passing. There was a faint sound that got drowned in the din of a passing train.

'Ghatchhh . . .'

That was the sound of my leg getting chopped. There was no one to hear my intense scream despite the deathly silence that followed after the train, completely unmoved by my plight, crossed me. I lay motionless for a while, watching the red blinking tail light of the train until it dimmed and faded into the darkness.

Then I passed out.

seconds, before gravitational force pulled me down. I thud-landed perilously close to the railway track. Despite my efforts, my left leg fell on the track over which one of the trains was still passing. There was a faint sound that got drowned in the din of a passing train.

'Khatchh!'

That was the sound of my leg getting chopped. There was no one to hear my intense scream despite the deathly silence that followed after the trains completely unmoved by my plight, crossed me. I lay motionless for a while, watching the red blinking tail light of last train until it dimmed and faded into the darkness.

Then I passed out.

I HAVE NEVER REALLY UNDERSTOOD WHY TRACK-SIDE spaces during morning hours turn into mass open toilets, where many prefer to defecate. I know that many parts of the state still lack proper toilets. Still the preference to answer the call of nature along the tracks always surprises me. Probably rural people visit them thinking that they are usually a little distance from their busy villages and hence safe for such private calls. That then is what I see as a great paradox. Not wanting to be seen with one's pants down in front of known faces is understandable. But what these simple folks probably don't realize is that by sitting near the tracks, they are only exposing themselves to the world. Trains carry population at times more than that of an entire village. Almost everyone who has travelled by train would have witnessed how red-faced villagers turn their backs when a train crosses them. Things are improving though.

But, I wasn't complaining at the moment. The lack of awareness or availability of toilets in this part of the state proved to be a blessing. A youth was apparently scouting for a suitable place to 'settle down' when he noticed me. I couldn't see his reactions but I could guess his predicament. Poor soul! He was about to relieve himself when he was apparently taken aback by the sight of a blood-soaked girl by the side of the track. Curiosity led him to take a couple of steps towards me, but then fear and 'morning pressure' perhaps forced him to turn and hurry away.

I had surprised myself by holding on for so long after so much blood loss. The youth had arrived as a ray of hope, which vanished as suddenly as it had appeared. Now, I was beginning to doubt how far I could go, lying by the side of the track, constantly losing blood, energy and even hope. I was beginning to question my fate when I saw a group of anxious-looking villagers coming towards me. The youth who had first spotted me had alerted several of his mates, all of whom arrived wearing a quizzical look.

Soon enough, there were a good number of people

beside me, each taking turns to see me from up close as if I was an alien who had landed on earth for the first time. '*Jinda hai ki mar gayi?* (Is she alive or dead?),' I heard them whisper among themselves as they stared at me from various angles. In the background I could hear the sound of women twisting their lips to make the 'tchh tchhh' sound to convey their sympathy. But I didn't need lip service. I needed someone to take me to the nearest hospital. And I was feeling cold too.

I saw a woman draped in what appeared like a cotton shawl or a blanket. Barely able to speak, I gestured at her to drape me in it. The woman understood what I was asking for. Yet she appeared reluctant and understandably so. She wasn't rich. Poor peasants like her struggle to make two ends meet. A shawl or a drape is a prized possession, something one cannot easily part with. But perhaps moved by my plight, she shed her reluctance. I think it was a wonderful gesture, given the financial worries women like her have to contend with on a daily basis. Our villages are full of such people. In crisis, invariably strangers agree to help. There are some exceptions too, but by and large, people are clean and God-fearing. My being alive to narrate my story is proof of this.

'What's your phone number? Where do you live?'

The man who beat a hasty retreat after spotting me lying by the track-side before he returned with help too was an example of a simple villager who takes a 'conscience vote' when faced with a moral dilemma. I later learnt that his name was Pintu Kashyap. He was the man who asked me if I remembered the phone number of anyone in my family. Of course I did! But, my voice choked with emotion and energy loss. I had lasted this long solely on the basis of my willpower. But everything has its limits. My limit appeared to have been reached. I gestured at him to bring his ear closer to my lips so that I could whisper the number to him. He did as asked. I first gave the number of my mother. That was not reachable so I whispered the number of Sahib, as I referred to my brother-in-law, in Kashyap's ear.

The youth gave a 'missed call' on the number. To give a missed call in what was clearly an emergency situation didn't make much sense. I wonder if he gave a missed call to save a rupee; and it must have been because his phone was low on balance. Whatever be the reason, it did hurt – though I mustn't forget that I wouldn't have survived had these people not done what they did. Luckily, Sahib always makes it a point to return all calls, including those from unknown numbers.

When he called back, the youth told him about my condition. The briefing was all correct, except for the fact that he said I had lost both my legs in the accident. I wondered how this information was being received at my family's end. But the youth couldn't be blamed for thinking that I had actually lost both my legs. One of my legs was visibly run over by the train and hung limply from inside of my badly torn clothes; the other was battered, bruised, broken and bloody. It looked as good as a 'gone case'.

After the conversation the youth told me that Sahib had requested that I be transported to the nearest hospital and that he would set out for the place right away. The youth was also assured that the entire expenses incurred by him in shifting me to the hospital would be reimbursed and with interest. Though the villagers later refused to accept money for their help, it was a sensible move to offer such incentives. Money is indeed a great motivator. In fact, even top companies offer incentives to their moneyed employees to boost productivity. In that sense, money is a great leveller too, as everyone seems to need it all the time. The poor want it and the rich want it too. Accumulating a pot of gold for one's needs is okay. The problem begins when one gets driven solely by financial concerns. It's not uncommon for such people to head for the Himalayas in search of peace towards the end of their lives.

The sound of a handcart being moved around me broke my trance. I was lifted from the side of the track and was about to be shifted to the cart, when a train arrived. This was the first train since the morning. The villagers took me in their embrace to ensure that I didn't get propelled back on to the track due to the force that a train generates while it's in motion. After the train crossed us, I was transported to the Chaneti railway station. From there I was moved into the guard cabin of a Bareilly-bound train.

I remember, at the Chaneti station, that the crowd of curious onlookers had swelled considerably. Everyone was watching me with pity in their eyes. But strangely enough, despite me requesting people to give me water, no one noticed my gestures. They were busy staring wide-eyed at me, with their faces showing pity even though their actions didn't support their expressions. I got several 'tchh tchhhs' (that roughly means 'Oh, poor soul') instead!

The crowd probably didn't understand what I wanted. I wasn't very clear or audible by that time. Anyway, it didn't take me long to reach Bareilly station, where I was moved out from the guard cabin, placed on a stretcher and left on the platform for an endlessly long time. Again, a crowd surrounded me. I felt odd, embarrassed, and angry too at their stares of empty sympathy.

A lady doctor arrived at the station after a long while and did a quick examination. She scribbled something on paper and referred me to the Bareilly district hospital. No one bothered to ensure that I was moved out of the platform. I kept lying there for a couple of hours.

Had they forgotten that I was alive? Would they have treated my dead body in the same manner? In fact, I suspect that had I been dead, people would have granted more respect to the lifeless body. I couldn't help smile at the irony in our country where a dead body is accorded more respect than a live one! A policeman was standing nearby, and I asked him why I wasn't being taken to a hospital. He replied, *'Kagazi karyavahi.'* Meaning paperwork!

This term 'paperwork' would have meant nothing to

me if I had not experienced its side effects first hand. It's nothing but an excuse to ensure that one gets to save their skin by filling some sheets of paper correctly even if it means delaying emergency treatment to a victim. At long last, some people arrived and transported me on a tempo to the Bareilly district hospital where I was again subjected to the by-now predictable stares and preliminary inquiries.

A short while later I heard hospital staffers describe my medical condition as critical. 'Her left leg has to be urgently operated on below the knee. Surgical procedure also needs to be performed on a badly broken right leg. This is a very critical case and so we need to get going fast . . .' a hospital staffer was saying. He paused briefly and then continued, '. . . the only problem is that we don't have an anaesthetist!'

The plight of district hospitals is shocking. They lack sufficient doctors and trained nurses. They don't have proper surgical equipment and no blood bank to meet an emergency like mine. Even the hospital staff looked jaded. Our country's health care system needs an overhaul, especially in states like UP.

By now I had realized that I needed to say goodbye to my left leg. I decided that in case an anaesthetist wasn't available I would ask to be wheeled into the operation theatre without one. 'Sir, don't worry if you don't have an anaesthetist. Please go ahead with the operation without one,' I said. The shocked look on the hospital staff's face betrayed the fact that he hadn't ever come across a patient like me, who was willing to feel a knife cut into them without the safety net of anaesthesia. B.C. Yadav, the hospital pharmacist, told me that without anaesthesia the pain would be unbearable. 'It is a must to ensure that the patient doesn't suffer pain while the surgery is performed,' he tried to explain.

The pharmacist was making a valid point. But, my endurance limit had been substantially enhanced overnight. 'Yadavji, through the night I suffered far greater pain and survived. The conditions there were appalling. In comparison, things are much better now. So don't worry. Please arrange for the surgery. I am ready.' I had spoken with such confidence that its effect was visible on them. I again addressed their concern: 'Sir, please don't feel guilty. I can bear the pain. At least this time I will have the satisfaction of knowing that the pain is for my good.' Yadavji was a kind man. I won't ever forget him. It was he who first agreed to consider my request. He consulted his co-staffers and doctors who, after some discussion and a lot of persuasion, reluctantly agreed.

I had barely crossed one hurdle when another stared me in the face. There was an urgent requirement of willing blood donors. Though I needed several units of blood, the doctors wanted at least one unit before the surgery. Barring family and close friends, such donors are hard to get. You get professional donors but they do it solely for money. In any case, neither my family was around, nor friends. I was in no position to track professionals. But even if they were available, I had no money to pay them. Having survived so far, I had a feeling that somehow I would cross this hurdle too. I knew help would arrive from unexpected quarters.

So it happened.

It's not usual for hospital staff to be so moved by a victim's situation as to volunteer help. That's because every day these staffers come across various patients, some critically ill or injured. Many die before them. Sights that most of us find disturbing are a routine feature for them. Over time, hospital employees get so used to this that some are even accused of being insensitive. But this is one charge that won't stick when it comes to Yadavji. 'I will donate blood for you,' he had declared after coming to know that I had no one to fall back upon. Unlike politicians who make tall promises without ever bothering to fulfil them, Yadavji honoured his words. He promptly got someone to puncture his vein and as blood trickled out in tiny droplets from his body, sliding through the thin tube to be stored in a plastic bag, I felt a lump in my throat.

In a little under an hour the plastic bag had swelled appreciably. A little beep indicated that one unit of blood had been stored. Still holding cotton at the point where the needle had punctured his vein, Yadavji slowly got down from the bed. He saw me looking at him and walked up to me and placed a hand on my head and smiled. 'After donating blood one should keep the cotton over the puncture point for a while without rubbing it over,' he said. I smiled back. 'If you require something let me know,' he said as he disappeared into the hospital. Long after he was gone I kept thinking about him. After the accident, I met several good men, who went out of their way to help me. He was one among them.

Such people and their gestures are rare and you tend to remember them for life.

LIKE A LOYAL SOLDIER, THE SEVERED PORTION OF MY left leg had continued to tag along with me, glued by a faint slice of skin, till the Bareilly district hospital. Its time was up. I knew it had to leave me. But even though it had been run over by a train, it clung to me, as if saying that long associations don't end just like that. The association indeed was long. As a national-level volleyball player, I relied as much on my legs as my hands to play. I played various other sports too. And every time I kicked a ball or dribbled it or netted it or dodged my opponents, I did so secure in the belief that my legs would provide the speed, balance and agility that every sportsperson requires.

My legs came in quite handy for some non-sporting activities too. I used them quite generously to run away from my two brothers whenever I was caught plotting against them. Race for race, I matched my two brothers, running with them just as long as my father, who usually cycled ahead, wanted us to. As naughty kids we used to try dangerous stunts like walking along the edge of our boundary wall, simply because we loved seeing the look of disbelief in the eyes of others. I was supremely confident of my ability to strike a balance everywhere. To ensure healthy bones, each time I had a chicken or a mutton piece on my plate I ate not just the fleshy part but chewed away the bones too as I had heard somewhere that animal bones were the best source of calcium. In fact, I used to say with a lot of pride that my bones were made of steel.

In the age of 'thank you' cards and messages, it's surprising that one rarely takes out time to thank God for bestowing a fit and healthy body. Most of us never respect it enough. Like most people, I always took my legs for granted. Now we were headed towards the end. Though the right leg thankfully was to stay with me, it wasn't going to be the same either. I had gathered from the doctors that a rod was to be inserted in my right leg as several of my bones had been broken so badly that a regular plaster wouldn't help. I wondered how I would cope with this reality.

From time to time I also anxiously looked towards the entrance to check if my family had arrived. I knew they must have been on the way the moment they heard the news.

All of us have, to borrow a quote from Shelley, fallen on the thorns of life and bled. But instead of being weighed down by trying circumstances, we emerge stronger from our frequent trials. I don't know for how long I lapsed into the past. My mother was a health supervisor in a government primary health centre in Kudraha block of Basti district. She was diabetic and had worked hard to bring us up ever since our army man father was found drowned under mysterious circumstances in a pond outside our government quarters where we lived. Eight months after my father's mysterious death, we found the police knocking at our door. We realized then that our dark days had only just begun. The police had acted on a complaint from one of our close relatives, who had claimed that my mother, my eldest sister and the elder of my two brothers had had a hand in my father's mysterious death. I guess my name and that of my other brother Rahul didn't figure in the police report as we were far too young. Both of us were kids. I was six years old, Rahul, a year younger. It was apparent that the arrest of the elders in my family was part of a larger conspiracy to cripple us. The police knew this too.

Thankfully, after a brief investigation not much meat was found in the accusation and the charge died soon after. My mother, brother and sister were released on bail in twenty-two days. But, even today I get goosebumps when I recall the time my brother and I spent alone, crying and fending for ourselves. We had a cow that my father had purchased. When the people around us turned into animals, the cow looked after us, guarding the house, providing us milk that helped us survive. In fact, we were so frightened to enter our own house that we spent most of those days sitting outside, crying and sleeping next to the cow that guarded us during that period.

Even that cow had to be later sold off as some of the distant relatives and friends demanded that we part with it in exchange for their support in securing the acquittal of the family. Shortly after being released from jail, my mother was transferred to a primary health centre at Mehdawal, now part of Sant Kabir Nagar district. That was about a hundred kilometres from Kudraha. Ravi bhaiya, the older of the two brothers, who had put up a small shop with the help of some friends decided to stay back in Kudraha to take care of his new business. A year had passed since we had shifted to Mehdawal. From time to time he would visit us and was happy that his business had started picking up. We too shared his happiness.

But our happiness didn't last long.

Ravi bhaiya was murdered – betrayed by his own friends with whom he had set up the business. No one really knows why his friends murdered him. We geared up for another fight. After our father's death, we neither had the money nor the local connections to go after the assailants. But my mother decided to pursue the case, despite threats to her life as well as ours. We were too young to understand the trauma my mother must have undergone then. But today we realize that perhaps there is something in our bloodline that makes us battle injustice and fight pain in our own rustic way. My mother courageously fought on.

Time, the great healer that it is, continued to fly. Soon we gradually started forgetting our pain and tried smiling again. It wasn't easy. But then life has to move on. No matter how great a loss, time always heals the pain, even though the scars remain. We too were learning to cope with the tragedy. Happiness came back in our lives when the marriage of my eldest sister was settled. It was the best thing to happen for the family.

In our brother-in-law Om Prakash, whom we referred to as Sahib or Bhai sahib, we discovered a friend, philosopher and guide. He worked for the CRPF but spent a lot of time with us. Probably because he was employed with a paramilitary force where discipline and hierarchy mattered a lot, first my sister and then all of us, started calling him Sahib. Slowly, we started depending on him for all our family's major decisions. And it was natural that he would be the person I would call first in my darkest hour.

'Beta . . .'

I thought I heard someone call out to me. The voice seemed to be coming from somewhere close . . . very close . . .

'Beta . . .'

Someone seemed to be calling again even as I was still lost in my memories. My mind was in chaos – all kinds of thoughts vying with each other to gain my attention.

'Beta . . .'

The voice seemed to be coming from somewhere close, very close . . .

Jolted into awareness, I saw that the person who was calling out to me was B.C. Yadav. He was standing next to my bed, trying to wake me up from my stupor. 'Beta, we are now going to prepare you for the surgery. I hope you are ready,' he said with a touch of affection in his voice. I nodded in consent.

Certain relations blossom instantly. My extended family members back in Kudraha had conspired against us and got my mother, sister and brother behind bars on a fake charge. And here was a complete stranger who wanted me to live. Life is indeed a great teacher. In only a couple of hours a bond had developed between me and Yadavji.

He smiled and went away. After sometime he returned with some other hospital staff who started readying me for the surgery. The staff went about their job of cleaning me up with efficient, professional ease. Even the touch of cotton hurt. It began to dawn on me that I was about to watch them perform a surgical procedure on me, without anaesthesia, with absolutely no cover for pain. Word had spread within the hospital about my decision. People including some patients who were about to be discharged, their attendants, hospital staff and doctors all took turns to cheer me up. They had seen patients and victims before, some in probably even worse shape than me. But most such patients were usually wheeled in unconscious. Given the pathetic state of affairs at the hospital, I guessed that the very critical cases either didn't survive or were referred elsewhere.

I too would have been referred elsewhere had I not voiced my willingness to get the surgical procedure done quickly and at all costs. That's why I was getting so much attention and relatively better care. I wasn't trying to be different. No one enjoys pain. But hearing the hospital staff discuss my situation had left me in no doubt that a surgery was required urgently. I knew that if I hadn't offered myself to be operated immediately, I would have risked my entire leg and my life too. The risk of gangrene was real.

The jeans that I had been wearing had been removed by now. I was draped in a hospital blanket. The surgeons arrived carrying various surgical equipment and smiled at me. After that they got busy, first to formally cut off my left leg from below the knee and then follow it up with cutting, cleaning and stitching of the opening at the place from where the leg was cut. I closed my eyes and clutched the edge of the bed tightly as I felt the knife on my body. The surgery was more painful than I had imagined. The surgeons moved the knife as expertly through my skin, as a housewife moves a butter knife through a loaf of bread.

It took me time to adjust to this 'new pain'. To keep my mind engaged, I kept talking to myself throughout the procedure. Every now and then I would let out a silent scream, whenever the knife slit my skin open or when the doctors stitched the wounds. But I drew strength from the surgeons, who were sporting a completely detached look even as they went about performing the job. I wondered if they were as calm inside. Soon they amputated my left leg from just below my knee. I felt a lump in my throat.

Even during school farewells, I would get emotional. This was like bidding a final farewell to my own body part – my leg. The surgeons were still at work. They had handed over my amputated leg to an attendant who casually placed it right below my hospital bed. Having resigned myself to fate, I had lost track of time. The surgery must have taken a while. The doctors said it was successful and then retired, leaving me with a heavily bandaged left leg. I was physically exhausted and must have immediately fallen asleep after the surgery.

Soon after I woke up, I saw a dog visiting our ward! It was absurd, even shocking, that a dog could walk into a hospital but it did provide some comic relief. The 'visitor' didn't seem particularly interested in anything in the ward, until he focused in the direction of my bed. Driven by animal instinct, the dog quickly traced the place from where he smelt raw flesh and found my severed leg that lay lifeless just below me. He needed no invitation after that. As he began licking the 'leg piece' I shouted. Someone chased the dog away. That was easy.

Chasing those memories away is difficult, even today.

SAHIB ARRIVED WITH MY ELDEST SISTER LAXMI, AT last. She was fighting hard to control her tears. As if to console her, Sahib said, 'If God has let her stay alive, I think it's a message that he has some plans for her. Don't worry; she is going to make history.'

Shortly after, my brother and mother too arrived. Barring a tear or two that my mother heroically tried to conceal, my family dealt with the tragedy stoically. Without wasting much time, Sahib quickly checked up on my health status and asked the doctors what was to be done next. The doctors told him that I urgently required blood. He immediately got busy donating a unit of blood. Once he had done that he began to look for more donors. Since donors weren't easy to get, Sahib ignored medical advice to give an additional unit of blood. For this he had to use his persuasive skills.

'Do I look weak? Check my weight. I am sure that nothing is going to happen to me. Moreover, please realize that this is being done for a noble cause, to save someone's life without risking mine.' Very reluctantly, the doctors agreed. They were worried that, should something happen to him, they would be in the line of fire. Both the sides – Sahib and the doctors – had their reasons.

The doctors were worried. The medical fraternity wouldn't have appreciated such unconventional gestures of allowing people to donate two units of blood back to back. Sahib's line too was compelling. If he wasn't allowed to give the second unit of blood, who else would? There weren't many options available. Of the four persons who were present, Rahul, who had just arrived, was busy running around; my mother was a diabetic and my elder sister wasn't well. Sahib knew that time was crucial. So he went about his task in a typical soldier-like fashion. This is one trait that runs through the family. We never waste time in brooding over losses. Whenever faced with a crisis, we focus on what needs to be done to contain further damage.

When I saw them, despite the obvious discomfort,

pain and trauma, I felt a sudden wave of energy within me. Though the black clouds of doubt had still not melted away, seeing my family near me – especially my mother, who had really faced the world all by herself and survived – I felt better. I told myself, 'I am the daughter of a brave woman. I cannot give up the fight. I will survive. I will win this battle for my mother.' After this 'inner connect', I realized it was important to make sure that family remained optimistic about my ability and my resolve to overcome the tragedy.

I placed my hand on my mother's hand, both to give support and to receive it. The sight of me lying in a hospital bed in this horrible state had devastated the family. While I needed their support, they required me to stay strong. They were drawing strength from me as I was from them. I saw Sahib and Rahul talking to each other. I could barely hear them but I think I guessed what they were speaking about – my future. Both sported an all-is-well look to reassure me. They later confessed that while on their way to the Bareilly hospital, they had thought – no, wished – that I was dead. I understood why they had made such a wish. My family had always known me to be a fearless, naughty, cheeky girl, playful and restless; cracking jokes, playing pranks or busy taking on even male players in sports like volleyball and football. To visualize me crippled for the rest of my life sent shivers down their spine.

However, Sahib had also prophesied that if I survived the trauma, it merely indicated that God had something in mind and that I may well go on to create history. These words gave me a lot of encouragement even though I was still uncertain how things were going to shape up. I remember snapping at Rahul when he got emotional. He was standing next to me, teary-eyed, when I saw him. Rahul didn't look me in the eye. He acted as if he was responsible for my tragedy. I knew this wasn't a good sign. I had known my younger brother to be a fearless character, whose vast energy reserves helped him work for longer hours without getting tired.

For my mother, he was an asset. After the mysterious death of my father Harendra Kumar Sinha and the murder of my brother Ravi, Rahul was – apart from Sahib – the only male in our close-knit family, who could be trusted, especially in such a crisis. It was important to ensure that he wasn't infected with 'the virus of negativity'. We needed to remain cheerful so that we could overcome the crisis. For that we needed to adopt a positive outlook and think of how to come out of this tragic situation, rather than be weighed down by it. That's why I was cross with Rahul when he showed signs of breaking down. 'Don't behave like a fool. Go and find out from the doctors how I can walk again!'

Rahul wasn't unhappy at having been admonished. It pumped him up. His eyes betrayed how happy my brother was to see me react like the 'good old fighter Sonu' as before. A smile crossed his lips as he looked at me with brotherly affection. I returned the smile. The family drew strength from our exchange. This was for them a confirmation that despite losing a leg, my fighting spirit was still intact. I hugged my mother and deliberately remained in her tight embrace for a touch longer than usual.

In the background, I heard the doctors tell Sahib that they had seen several patients but none as gutsy and determined as me. 'She is a special girl,' I heard the doctors say.

THIS IS THE AGE OF OB VANS.

It would have been unimaginable a decade or two back for an ordinary girl's trauma to shake up the collective consciousness of an entire country. Of course, to make it to breaking news you need to have a good story and a touch of luck too. Fortunately, I had both. Sahib had spotted a local photojournalist from the Hindi daily *Hindustan* near the Bareilly district hospital inside which I lay. Showing remarkable presence of mind, he approached the photojournalist to tell him my story and deliberately dropped the 'she is a national player' hint to catch the interest of the photo man. In today's time, merely having 'content' isn't enough. You need to know the art of marketing it too. Sahib was a skilled marketing man. He never played with facts. It was just that he sold those facts in such an engaging way to arouse curiosity. My story was published on page two of the newspaper's Bareilly edition. Sahib knew that it would not remain a Bareilly-centric story. He had predicted that the news would go national. The paper's English edition – *Hindustan Times* – also covered the story.

That was the trigger.

Influential local politicians started arriving. There was the Bareilly mayor Supriya Aron, the former Bharatiya Janata Party (BJP) MP and former union minister from Bareilly Santosh Gangwar, influential BJP leader from the region Maneka Gandhi among others. All of them said nearly similar things, expressing solidarity, promising help, blaming the system. Sahib was right. From page two, my story moved to page one of most newspapers. I was prime-time TRP material now. That was enough reason for channels to begin parking their OB vans outside the hospital.

The story of a national-level volleyball player being thrown out of a moving train while fighting chain snatchers in UP, where everything invariably is linked to politics and all blame heaped on the doorstep of the party in power, was a sure shot TRP grosser. The fact that Uttar Pradesh had a woman Chief Minister then at the helm of affairs meant that till such time as bigger and more happening news arrived, I would stay on the TV screens. In Sahib, they found a compelling and fearless narrator too. Channels thrive on moving visuals and juicy bytes. The visuals of me on a hospital bed were moving enough, and Sahib's talk was packed with punches. He ensured that I shed my reluctance to ask the media with their cameras if this should be the fate of national-level women players. I also said that it was time that the governments woke up to the security of women on trains and off it.

Soon everyone across the country knew all there was to know about the incident. The channels repeatedly ran the story, complete with my byte and Sahib's accusations. Breaking news is infectious. After one channel begins relaying it, others make a dive for it too. Some of them started doing live shows from outside the Bareilly district hospital, inside which I lay, feeling a little amused. I took some time to come to terms with TV crews working round the clock to ensure that they covered me from all angles. I remember some of them even waking me up at night to get a 'byte'. I understood their compulsions too. Having unleashed a storm, even they perhaps were helpless as my story had begun to create a national outcry.

As the live images of me in a hospital bed telling my story started invading drawing rooms, intensifying public curiosity and concern, the news channels stepped up the coverage. Soon my privacy began to get encroached upon. But I also knew that the media persons, who had started camping at Bareilly from across the country, were on the job 24x7 to ensure that they didn't miss out on any development. Many of them were doing so many live shows, feeds and phone-ins that they went hungry for hours. Sucked into a media storm, I wondered where it would take me. Thankfully the impact of the blitzkrieg was positive. I started getting better treatment, more personalized care with some 'big' doctors beginning to visit me.

The channel reporters told us that the prime minister was on a tour of China where he was quizzed about my incident. The PM had reportedly got in touch with his railway minister on the issue. The Congress chief Sonia Gandhi too was reportedly informed about my case. A flurry of political activity followed. The UP assembly polls were due in February 2012. Politicians of all major political parties were busy making themselves accessible to the common man, lest they be dubbed as elitist, an image that all politicians want to avoid especially in the run-up to a crucial election.

So everyone who heard my story started visiting me or sending their representatives across. Top officials were now being asked by politicians to visit me. I remember being woken up at around 2.30 a.m. by Sahib who informed me that the chairman of the Railway Board was arriving with senior officers to record my statement. After completing the official formalities the high-profile delegation explained the reason for waking me up at this hour.

'The issue is to be listed on the rail agenda tomorrow morning. The minister Mamata Banerjee is rushing from West Bengal to chair the meeting,' an official explained. He said, 'Rail minister has accorded top-most priority to this. She has even decided to cut short her campaign for the West Bengal assembly elections to chair this meeting in which she might make some major announcement for you.'

Next day a State Women's Commission member visited me to give a draft of Rs 1 lakh from the UP government and promised that the entire cost of treatment would be borne by the then Bahujan Samaj Party (BSP) government in the state. UP's transport minister, Ram Achal Rajbhar, sent Rs 51,000 through the Assistant Regional Transport Officer, Bareilly, who apologized for the minister not being able to make it as he was away and promised that Rajbharji would visit me as soon as he was free.

The same day, the then state chief of the Samajwadi Party Akhilesh Yadav who had begun campaigning for the UP assembly elections visited me. 'You have been very brave. We are proud of you. Tell me if there is anything that I can do for you,' he asked. After a brief pause, even as I gathered myself to speak to him, he said, 'I am giving you Rs 1 lakh right now from the party fund. Please tell me if you need anything else.'

I don't really know what made me say it but I demanded his assistance for setting up a sports academy for the handicapped. Probably it was divine intervention. A major project had just been conceived without any formal discussion. Akhilesh Yadav promised that if his party got to form its own government in UP, he would help. 'We won't forget our promise, as politicians usually do,' he said with a little smile playing on his lips. Overcome with joy at the young politician's disarming smile and honest conversation, I blurted out, 'Bhaiya, I think you are going to be the next chief minister!'

Those words proved to be prophetic but I remember being admonished by Sahib for speaking without even thinking. For at that time, even though many expected the Samajwadi Party to do well, it was Akhilesh's father Mulayam Singh Yadav who was widely tipped to be the next CM. When we were kids, my mother used to tell me that at certain times of the day Goddess Saraswati – who is supposed to bestow knowledge and learning – comes to stay with the individual. During that period, whatever one says turns out to be true. What I had said on an impulse later turned out to be true. Mulayam Singh Yadav decided to relinquish his claim for the CM's post in favour of heir apparent and son Akhilesh, who had brilliantly shared his father's load during the campaign. It was junior Yadav who had connected with the youth, who voted decisively in favour of the Samajwadis. After Akhilesh Yadav became the state's chief minister, he feted me besides giving a cheque of Rs 25 lakh for a 'mountain of a feat' about which I will discuss a little later in this book. He also gave me an additional Rs 1 lakh for my 'personal expenses' which I was a little reluctant to accept. But the genial CM insisted that I accept it. His gesture touched me. Politicians are known to make tall promises before elections but only rarely tend to follow up afterwards. Akhilesh Yadav had arrived on UP's political scene like a breath of fresh air.

'WHAT?' I COULDN'T BELIEVE MY EARS. THE INJECTION that the doctors at the Bareilly hospital had just prescribed for me was going to cost Rs 25,000! That was, for a family like ours, a lot of money. The doctors had said that it was essential to get the injection to prevent gangrene, a potentially life-threatening condition caused by death of body tissue. But it was not to be found in Bareilly either. Rather it had to be procured from Moradabad, famous for its brass work, a couple of hours away from Bareilly. Sahib knew that if he went to fetch it himself, it would mean leaving me alone with my ill sister. So he contacted a local medicine seller and persuaded him to get the injection. The medicine seller wasn't driven by altruism. He agreed to get the injection only after being promised that he would get a little extra money for his effort.

When Sahib had set out for Bareilly, he had had Rs 65,000 in his bank account, of which some had been spent in hiring a taxi to Bareilly and now a heavy chunk had just gone towards procuring the injection. Our financial condition continued to remain grim even after the arrival of my mother and brother. Shocked by my news, they had travelled general class from the first available train without remembering to arrange for cash. They weren't to be blamed either.

A daughter's relationship with her mother is always a special one. Unlike a male child, whose bond with his mother usually develops until puberty before dipping as he becomes weighed down by the pressures of marriage and work, a girl's relationship with her mother grows and cements with time. Even though girls too get busy with husband and children, they remain connected to their mother, for love and moral support. A mother, whose daughter had set out for a big city for a job interview and is found nearly dead by the railway track track, will naturally be in a tearing hurry to be by her daughter's side. That was why when she reached me with my brother she had just Rs 3000 with her. That was obviously not going to be enough.

Plastic money is still, by and large, an urban-India

phenomenon. Rural areas are fast getting ATMs but even today villagers mostly prefer to carry cash over a card. So here we were, all huddled together in my hospital room, plagued with doubt and wondering about what lay inside future's womb – a fresh opportunity or a mountain of trouble. None of us spoke much yet we conversed silently; our tear-filled eyes doing most of the talking. We had got some help from the politicians but we knew it wouldn't be enough. It was clear I was going to need expensive treatment. The first challenge was to arrange for enough cash that would ensure that my treatment didn't get affected. But a bigger and immediate challenge was to catch some sleep. Our eyelids were turning heavy. When body parts start sending such signals, we don't have a choice but to listen to them. We closed our eyes, each one of us unable to shut out our worries.

The same night we had a unique visitor. He introduced himself as Uma Shankar Dixit, 60, a resident of Unnao, near Kanpur. Dixitji came with monetary help of Rs 21,000. The light was so dim that we could hardly see his face nor count the money he was offering for my treatment. 'Please get some medicines for the girl,' he said. He said he had come to know about my tragedy through the media and couldn't control himself from driving down 400 km in his jeep to meet me. 'My daughter has sent me here,' he said in response to our queries on what led him to take such a long journey.

We needed the money. In fact we required more such people. My family requested Dixitji to give the amount in front of the media so that more people could offer help. Dixitji refused, saying he would prefer to remain anonymous. But he made an offer to me. 'I have heard that you desire to set up a sports academy for the handicapped. I wish you well. After you recover and decide to set up the academy near Unnao, please let me know. I would provide you bricks for your noble project free of cost,' he said.

He then gave us his mobile number and good wishes before disappearing into the night.

BAREILLY DISTRICT HOSPITAL DOCTORS AND OTHER staff had done their best. But it was now time to bid adieu and leave Yadavji and the other hospital staff who had taken good care of me. I required specialized treatment now. And Akhilesh Yadav, the Samajwadi Party leader, had suggested Lucknow's trauma centre as an option. That is where we intended to go.

My two and a half days' stay at Bareilly had been quite eventful. I had entered the Bareilly district hospital as a regular victim but now, thanks to the 24x7 media, the country was following me and sending me their good wishes. On 14 April when I headed for Lucknow in an ambulance, media vans followed me. The road ride was bumpy. Every now and then I would cry out in pain as every jerk would make blood seep through the stitches that were still very raw.

My family was constantly telling the ambulance driver to go slow but even he was helpless on such roads. After four hours of a painful drive, during the course of which several of my stitches split open, we finally arrived at Lucknow's trauma centre and I was admitted to the general ward.

I would have continued to be treated in a routine way had the media teams not begun assembling outside the trauma centre. As the TV channels and OB vans lined up outside the hospital, some beginning to beam news of my arrival here, the King George's Medical University (KGMU) administration hurriedly banned the media from entering the campus.

The KGMU bosses explained that media entry was being banned in the interest of the patients. Nobody can argue with the line that patients need complete privacy and silence. Media entry and the ensuing chaos could have disturbed that. But was that the real reason for taking such a step? I guess in most government hospitals things are far from ideal. There is a shortage of everything. And news cameras generally don't miss anything. After some time due to media pressure I was soon moved to the VVIP ward. This ward, we learnt later, is usually maintained for top politicians, bureaucrats and other influential people.

While the state of affairs in the general ward was shocking, the VVIP ward was a study in contrast. It appeared to me like a top-of-the-line hotel, with neat beds, spick and span rooms, properly clean and shining toilets and a courteous staff willing to serve with a pleasing smile.

Despite the ban, the media continued to keep people updated on any development that was related to me. Due to the relentless onslaught of the press, visitors – both VIPs and commoners – started visiting me. They included ministers, bureaucrats, social activists, Page-3 people, builders, engineers, sportspersons along with the ubiquitous aam aadmi.

The then BSP government rushed several of its ministers like Ayodhya Pal and Ram Achal Rajbhar among others to meet me and offer their support and sympathy. Rajbhar's aides had also contacted me at the Bareilly district hospital through their representatives to extend monetary help. A CISF deputy commandant led a group of soldiers to the hospital. All of them donated blood to me. Several NGO workers and social activists too arrived. Many of them offered financial help. For instance, a social activist and sports enthusiast T.P. Havelia gave me Rs 5100.

My popularity had grown significantly in the last couple of days. And the media's continued interest in me ensured that the KGMU administration was on its toes all the while. Every now and then some VIP would visit me and many of them would even tell the doctors and staff to take 'proper care' of me. While the VIPs were offering me, in that order, lip service, sympathy and a little cash, their presence meant that the KGMU bosses were always being served timely reminders of my 'special' status, one that would ensure that there was no dip in the level of treatment.

By now the surgeons in the hospital had performed a second surgery on my left leg. Right now all focus was on my left leg. My right was still untouched. KGMU doctors were hopeful that after my operation and an artificial limb I would be able to lead a near-normal life. Government hospitals are usually choking with patients and thus the doctors often get used to treating them in a certain way that many find despicable. But I say with experience that if you can tap some connections, then the level of diagnosis the government doctors can provide remains unmatched. That's simply because over a period of time, the sheer volumes help doctors perfect their diagnosis. Meanwhile, I continued to get visitors.

Till now, while I had been told by media persons in Bareilly that my case had attracted the attention of the country's most powerful, I wasn't actually aware of what was happening in Delhi until the then Uttar Pradesh Congress Committee chief Rita Bahuguna Joshi visited me. She told me that the then union sports minister Ajay Maken would be visiting here soon on the instructions of Congress chief Sonia Gandhi and Prime Minister Manmohan Singh. The minister arrived couple of hours later.

He had also brought with him a team of doctors from Delhi's famed All India Institute of Medical Sciences (AIIMS). He patiently heard me and my family narrate the sequence of events that led me here, checked up on my medical status and asked the doctors how long the treatment would take. After some time he got up to leave. 'If you agree, we can arrange for your treatment at AIIMS. There is no urgency. You can take your time to think it over,' he said as he left. Two surgeries had been performed on me so far. But still my treatment was far from over. I required sustained medical attention for several months. Maken had left the ward by now. He was, in fact, on his way out of the hospital along with a retinue of political workers, police and media.

We were in a fix. The KGMU administration was offering excellent care. There was no reason to complain. In Lucknow we had an advantage as most of our friends and relatives were either in the state capital or nearby. Our financial position was still pitiable. That's why the family was in two minds over the offer to move to Delhi for treatment, where we knew nobody. We would have continued to debate endlessly had a woman journalist from a Hindi newspaper *Dainik Jagran* not given us some valuable and very timely advice.

'Right now the iron is hot. So you must take the Delhi offer. AIIMS is a far better hospital than the one in Lucknow. Above all, you do not know what may happen once the media lowers its interest in the case. And you know that even the media won't be able to sustain pressure endlessly,' she said to my family, adding, 'Right now the entire country is with you. Please don't play with Arunima's future.'

Sahib who was talking to the journalist was impressed with the advice. The family went into a huddle and after a quick check we were ready. Like all the big decisions in my family, this too was taken quickly – in only thirty seconds! Maken after making the 'Delhi offer' had almost reached his red-beaconed vehicle. As one of his staff opened the rear door of the vehicle to let him in, Sahib made a dash for the minister, shouting, 'Sir . . . sir' at the top of his voice. Curious, Maken turned around to discover a virtually out-of-breath Sahib announce, 'Sir, we are ready . . . ready to go to Delhi!'

The minister responded positively to his request. 'Very well then, I will make all the arrangements for you. Now, get ready fast.' His cool manner and the efficiency with which he went about completing the task assigned to him impressed everyone in the family. Maken informed the Uttar Pradesh Congress Committee chief to arrange for my discharge from the hospital and got busy calling up the home secretary to ensure availability of an air ambulance to fly me to Delhi. In the next sixty minutes, I was moved from the KGMU bed to an ambulance that took me to the airport and from there into an air ambulance that flew me to Delhi. I was moved from the hospital to the airport in a cavalcade that also comprised the district magistrate, top police officers and media vans.

The entire road from the hospital to Lucknow airport was cleared during the journey. My family was telling me about all this and even though I lay weak inside the ambulance, I felt good. I had seen in the news how celebrities like film stars and sportspersons were feted at the airport and crowds jostled to catch a glimpse of their favourite stars or players. Never in my wildest dreams had I imagined that people would gather for me too. At the Delhi airport, as the stretcher on which I lay was brought out from the air ambulance, I could see couple of thousand people having gathered to greet me.

My being shifted from Lucknow to Delhi for treatment on the intervention of the PM and the Congress chief was 'big breaking news'. I realized later that, for the media and many others who came for live discussions in TV studios, my being moved from Lucknow to Delhi had a political context too. While UP was under BSP rule, the Congress-led government was ruling at the centre. Since the UP assembly polls were due, my accident had got linked to politics. I was oblivious to the political ramifications of my shifting. Some friends and family claimed later that

UP government officials had advised them against my opting for Delhi, saying I would get the best treatment in Lucknow itself.

It was indeed true that the facilities at the VIP ward at the trauma centre in Lucknow were very good. There was no apparent need to shift to Delhi. But the advice of the lady journalist who was covering my story for a Hindi paper also appeared wise. So we opted for Delhi though our decision was not inspired by any political motive. Little did we know that we would soon be sucked into a controversy; my character and conduct questioned and my family targeted; wrong motives attributed to virtually everything about and around me.

But at the moment, amid flashes, mikes and TV cameras, as I was moved past a maze of journalists, busy beaming live images of me, into a waiting ambulance that drove me to AIIMS, we had no inkling of any of this. Even if we had had, there was little we could have done about it. My ambulance had reached AIIMS and Maken was there to greet and guide us along with some local politicians. Nearly all of those present there knew Maken well, including two influential real estate, Ramesh Sikka and Dharamvir Bharti.

These two, we gathered later, had come there on

Maken's instructions. Both were courteous to a fault. Soon it became clear why Maken had asked them to be present when we arrived at AIIMS. They were asked to look after us during our Delhi stay, a task they performed to perfection. They became our local contact and resource persons in Delhi. While I was at AIIMS, my family stayed at their guest house, where they were provided VIP facility for free.

Even more striking was the fact that not once did anyone at the guest house make it appear as if they were doing us a favour by hosting us for free and for so long. Whenever I found hospital food boring, they ensured that proper home-cooked food was sent to me. Even a fresh set of clothes for Sahib and my brother Rahul were arranged by them after the AIIMS administration warned them that they would be banned from entering the hospital unless they took a bath and changed. Sahib hadn't changed his clothes for ten days and it was only after AIIMS staff told him to do so, did he agree. My immediate family was so busy taking care of me that no one had the time to even think of what clothes one was wearing or if one had even brushed one's teeth. Sahib later told me that he brushed his teeth after ten days!

Because of Maken and the people to whom he

had entrusted the responsibility of ensuring my care, we didn't face any real problem in Delhi. The union minister knew the state of mind of a family in distress and was always very polite while talking to me. I was put up at the Commonwealth Games ward, set up for the Commonwealth Games that were held in Delhi. It was a state-of-the-art ward. If Lucknow's VIP ward at the trauma centre had appeared like a hotel, the one in Delhi resembled a five-star hotel. The spick-and-span ward, immaculately dressed ward boys, tidy nurses sporting a pleasing smile – all were a welcome surprise. A soothing fragrance hung in the air.

If the entire country were to have such hospitals, the patient recovery rate would certainly be much faster. I knew it was too much to expect in a state where the maternal and infant mortality rate was among the highest in the country. Unfortunately such hospitals are few and far between. For most Indians, wards like the one I was put up in remain a dream. For a below-middle-class Indian like me, even a day's charge – stay and treatment – in wards like these would be equal to our annual earnings. The entire family wanted the best treatment for me, but knew that even if they were to sell all their movable and immovable assets they would still not be able to raise enough to meet even half of the total expense incurred on my treatment.

Thankfully Ajay Maken had taken care of this aspect. He had informed the AIIMS director that the union government would foot the entire cost of my treatment. Maken asked the director to get an estimate prepared and present it to him at the earliest. We were greatly relieved to hear the minister tell AIIMS authorities that my treatment would be completely free. A team of dedicated doctors started treating me. There were nurses as well as ward boys round the clock. I was given personal numbers of several senior AIIMS staffers, in case of an emergency. A steady stream of visitors kept flowing in throughout my AIIMS stay.

Some of the visitors I met insisted that I accept donations they had collected to fund my treatment. They were obviously unaware that the treatment was being completely funded by the union government. We politely declined all monetary help. Despite our repeated requests they insisted that we accept their contribution. 'If not for your treatment then please accept it as a token of our support for the sports academy that you have in mind,' they said. I marvelled at the level of their interest in me and whatever I had said.

Soon the AIIMS administration began issuing daily medical bulletins on my status. I was told that young people, auto drivers, roadside vendors were carrying out candle marches to galvanize support for me and to pray for my recovery. Were they related to me? Did they share some kind of cosmic connection with me? All of them belonged to the below-poverty-line category. An auto driver or a roadside vendor cannot afford to waste time. For them time is money. Yet, they were the ones now in the forefront of a campaign to galvanize support for a total stranger. All this gave me a lot of emotional satisfaction. Along with the best and latest equipment and technology that was used for my treatment by the AIIMS administration, such selfless gestures of the aam aadmi were really very reassuring.

Slowly I started responding to the treatment.

at the level of their interest in me and whatever I had said?

Soon the AIIMS administration began issuing daily medical bulletins on my status. I was told that young people, auto drivers, roadside vendors were carrying out candle marches to galvanize support for me and to pray for my recovery. Were they related to me? Did they share some kind of cosmic connection with me? All of them belonged to the below-poverty-line category. An auto driver or a roadside vendor cannot afford to waste time. For them time is money. Yet they were the ones now in the forefront of a campaign to galvanize support for a total stranger. All this gave me a lot of emotional satisfaction. Along with the best and latest equipment and technology that was used for my treatment by the AIIMS administration, such selfless gestures of the aam aadmi were really very reassuring.

Slowly I started responding to the treatment.

AN UNUSUALLY DRESSED WOMAN, DECKED UP IN loads of jewellery, her hair tied up in extraordinarily huge bunch-like formations and wearing costly rings and heavy make-up, made a dramatic entry in my ward one day. 'Hello, I am Shahnaz Hussain,' she introduced herself fluttering her large eyes on which she had applied a thick layer of kohl.

Her aides kept working on her hair, ensuring her jewellery rested properly on her dress. She exuded warmth and positivity, smelt nice and indicated her preference for doing things big. After some time she told me the reason that had brought her to me. 'I have come to make you an offer. If you want we can train you as a beautician here in the hospital itself. Armed with my international diploma, you can go and set up a Shahnaz Hussain franchisee. It would help you stand on your own legs after you recover,' she said.

Shahnaz Hussain is a big name in the fashion and beauty world. Her beauty products are available everywhere. All of us agreed that an international diploma from Hussain would certainly be helpful. So we didn't take long in accepting her offer. The AIIMS administration, however, wasn't amused at the idea of a patient learning beauty tips on her hospital bed. It turned down Shahnaz Hussain's request.

The beautician who wore extraordinarily large earrings also knew big people. She pulled strings and a short while later had managed to get the AIIMS administration to allow me to be trained inside the VIP Commonwealth Games ward. Though Shahnaz had done all this to help me, I couldn't help think how easy it is for some in this country to break the rules or bend the system. I started learning beauty tips through a tutor and a principal Shahnaz had arranged. My elder sister too decided to learn beauty techniques and thus both of us were imparted training on how to become successful and professional beauticians.

We practised on dummies. By the time I was discharged from AIIMS, I had become a certified diploma holder and was authorized to set up a franchise. Along with my sister, I cleared the beauty training examination in the hospital itself. This training helped me divert attention from my pain and drive away worries about my future. In the meantime, the surgeons had tirelessly worked on my legs to ensure that I achieved a certain level of confidence in my ability to walk again, even if on an artificial left leg. Medical bulletins were being issued regularly for the media which kept following me and the progress that I was making at AIIMS.

As I thought that things were getting better, criticism started surfacing against me in the media. Inexplicably, the Government Railway Police (GRP), Bareilly had begun to question the sequence of events that led to me losing a leg. The excellent treatment I had started receiving and the kind of response I was getting from across the country had apparently not gone down well with some acquaintances. They were the ones who helped the GRP give a new twist to the whole episode. They sent anonymous letters to them alleging that I had a dubious past. Allegations ranged from wild to wicked and were splashed all across the newspapers. The letters that were sent to the GRP contained a bundle of lies. From travelling without a ticket, to having an affair, to jumping off the train in an attempt to commit suicide, to Sahib pushing me out of the train, to travelling illegally on the footboard from which I fell due to a jerk, to having been attacked elsewhere and thrown by the railway tracks and not being a national-level player. The same media that had stood behind me and supported me was used to spread vicious lies against me. Every day new charges would be levelled against me. All of a sudden I was being portrayed as an opportunistic girl, who was out to garner money and sympathy too. Newspapers and TV channels branded me as a girl of easy virtue and my family members were variously described as murderers and even rapists.

The GRP wanted to save its skin. An impartial inquiry would have nailed them. Since security on trains was the GRP's duty and my incident had put it in the dock, the railway cops were out to prove me wrong. They had ensured that all criticism against me was properly carried in the media. It wasn't very difficult to guess who those people were and why they were doing so. But, no matter how rational one tries to appear, a volley of criticism, thrown at you without any warning, is bound to leave you rattled. You do need time to recover from such unprovoked assaults on one's character. How would you react if suddenly, without any reason, someone you have never met or interacted with only rarely, arrived at your office and rudely asked you to clear your debt? Your initial reaction would be of shock and disbelief, wouldn't it?

Even when you recover, it won't be easy to offer a credible defence. That's because no one can defend an outrageous charge, at least not immediately. One can get violent or use intemperate language in anger but that is used to brand you as someone who is not just undisciplined but a compulsive liar or even a fraud who gets aggressive when confronted with uncomfortable facts. What's more, there is a strong chance that even your colleagues will start doubting you. That's why I was terribly hurt with all these accusations and started losing hope. This is probably exactly what the conspirators had aimed for. Breaking my self-confidence was their first target. They would have succeeded too, had my family members not begun countering the allegations with proof.

'Come on. Such things are bound to happen. Don't get disheartened. Such tactics are proof that we are on the right track,' my family said. My family started answering these allegations 'with proof'. Though I had lost my plastic bag containing my certificates and my cell phone in the accident, the ticket that I had purchased from the turbaned Sikh who was on the booking counter of the Lucknow railway station was still intact in my backpack. Subsequent railway inquiries exposed the hollowness of the claim that I was travelling on the footboard of the general compartment and fell. If Sahib had indeed pushed me, it would have been impossible for him to hire a prepaid taxi from Lucknow to Bareilly to reach me. The timing of his hiring the taxi from Lucknow was on record. It was absurd that the GRP, Bareilly was accusing Sahib of having pushed me out of the train even as he hired a Lucknow–Bareilly taxi from the prepaid GRP taxi booth in the state capital. Once again we relied on the media to express our views. As the media began relaying our rejoinders and rebuttals, the opposition, which included some senior officials in the then UP government and some acquaintances, started to backtrack.

They hadn't imagined that I would recover from their attack to launch a counter-offensive. My family stood solidly behind me. So did the union minister

Maken and those men who were entrusted with the responsibility of looking after us.

While one expects support from one's family in a crisis, it was the behaviour of Maken and his men that was most pleasing. It would have been very easy for them to disown me, saying that I was now discredited. But, they had seen me from close up. I am of the firm opinion that even though you may not know everything about a person in the first couple of meetings, if one is observant enough you will get a basic idea of what a person is like. A person who has got nothing to hide definitely exudes a certain kind of innocence, one that instantly appeals.

Perhaps the minister and his men, who knew the ways of the world, had realized that my story was a credible one, not cooked up to gain sympathy as some insinuated. I really enjoyed that live TV debate in which Sahib was also invited. The debate was focused on the accusations against me and if there was any truth behind those claims. A senior police official alleged that my family and I were trying to gain sympathy by hyping the tragedy, which he claimed was self-inflicted. The TV anchors sought a response from Sahib to the accusation against me. Since the charge was made by a senior IPS officer, it needed to be countered effectively.

Sahib's response was precise, right on the money. He said, 'Sir, if you feel Arunima is trying to gain sympathy by marketing her tragedy, I would suggest that you too get your leg chopped off to do so. You are well connected. The media will come to you and then you can get several benefits as your story would then travel far and wide!' The reply must have stung. Not surprisingly, the IPS officer soon left the TV debate midway saying that we were 'uncouth'! That was very satisfying! I was regularly targeted – my losing a leg, the fact that I was thrown out of the moving train by chain snatchers were all questioned.

What's more, despite being subjected to ridiculous accusations and weird charges, we were still expected to behave normally! Being poor doesn't just mean going to bed hungry; it also means being forced to live with shocking charges, outlandish claims, raised eyebrows and pointed fingers. I wanted to shout at the top of my voice: 'For God's sake, stop indulging in politics. I have lost a leg. The loss is real. I am ready to face any inquiry that can help establish that the sequence of events as narrated by me was correct.' At the same time I wanted those people who doubted my story and cast aspersions on me to be punished. I wanted them to prescribe a punishment for themselves, should they be proved wrong.

I could understand criticism but not a deliberate effort to malign me, to run me down and question me just because my truth was hurting some important people. Around the same time a Public-Interest Litigation (PIL) was filed in my case by Adarsh Mehrotra, a lawyer in the Allahabad High Court's Lucknow bench. The court, after hearing the issue, had directed the railways to pay a monetary compensation of Rs 5 lakh to me. The railways too hired a senior lawyer. But his arguments against me were dismissed by the high court. Each day offered new hope and fresh challenges. Every day I learnt something new. The pages on the calendar continued to move swiftly. We regularly updated ourselves with whatever was happening around the world through newspapers that we got in our VVIP ward.

One morning Sahib suddenly asked me, '*Everest chadogi?* (Will you climb Mt Everest?)' He had just read an interesting piece of information in the newspaper. While many had scaled the Everest, no female amputee had ever done so. I wasn't amused. 'I have lost a leg.

And you talk of Mt Everest!' Sahib smiled. 'That is precisely why I am talking of Everest,' he said. By now even I was beginning to see what Sahib was trying to get at. If I could take a shot at the Everest and succeed, I would become the first female amputee ever to have done so. Of course, it was a very tough task. Even inside my ward I had to walk with the support of my family. To even think of conquering the Everest appeared a distant dream. Sahib insisted that if I agreed and kept faith, I could make 'history'. It was at this moment that I recalled the wild allegations that were levelled against me.

The charge that I wasn't a national player still hurts. Conquering Everest, assuming I was able to do so, would be an ideal way to answer my critics. After Sahib contested the charges on camera and dared the GRP officials to a live TV debate, Delhi-based bosses of the Sports Authority of India (SAI) started conceding that I was indeed a national player. However, to our surprise they conceded the fact with a rider that 'while I was indeed a national player, the status would be conceded to me by the same department which would eventually give me a job'! There were several certificates with me that proved I was a national player. But when a person is plagued by doubt, nothing seems to work. Every now and then I would feel low.

This had continued for a while until the idea of Mt Everest came along. I conveyed to Sahib my willingness to take up the challenge. '*Theek hai, Hum karengey* (Okay, I will do it),' I said. I now had something to look forward to – a mission, a goal, a reason to dream. It was not going to be easy. But, throughout my life nothing had come easy. While I had scaled boundary walls before, for the first time I planned to test myself against a mountain. No female amputee had succeeded before. It was both a challenge and an opportunity. A glass is always either half full or half empty. How you look at it determines your approach to life. For me, and in fact for my whole family, no matter what happened, the glass was always half full. The effort was always on how to fill up the glass entirely. We should always live in hope.

I felt like I was being born again.

is plagued by doubt, nothing seems to work. Every now and then I would feel low.

This lull continued for a while, until the idea of Mt Everest came along. I conveyed to Sahib my willingness to take up the challenge. '*Theek hai, hum karenge*' ('Okay, I will do it'), I said. I now had something to look forward to—a mission, a goal, a reason to dream. It was not going to be easy. But throughout my life nothing had come easy. While I had scaled boundary walls before, for the first time I planned to test myself against a mountain. No female employee had succeeded before. It was both a challenge and an opportunity. A glass is always either half full or half empty. How you look at it determines your approach to life. For me, and in fact for my whole family, no matter what happened, the glass was always half full. The effort was always on how to fill up the glass entirely. We should always live in hope.

I felt like I was being born again.

I REALLY WANTED TO GET WELL SOON NOW. IN FACT, I started waiting anxiously for the day when I would get my artificial limb. When it finally arrived, I was overjoyed. I felt like dancing. What's more, the artificial leg felt almost like my real leg. In fact, I could hardly feel the difference. For me this was like a new lease of life. In my mind I had already begun to steel myself for taming Everest. I was very happy when my trainers, who were sent to help me get used to the artificial limb, announced that my training sessions were about to begin. They began coaching me on how to adjust to the foreign leg, how to walk, the precautions I was to take. After they had finished the day's session, my trainers would leave the artificial leg next to my bed. I would wear it again the next morning for a fresh training session.

I had started falling in love with this 'stranger' with whom I was wedded for life. But now, I wanted to try walking alone. I was surrounded by people who would instantly come to give me a helping hand to stop me from tripping over, every time I would leave my bed. I began to feel impatient. At night I felt restless and tossed and turned in bed. I couldn't share with anyone the inner turmoil I was experiencing. I also knew that no one other than me would be able to understand my agony. I had been through so much – suffered pain, battled conspiracy, survived personal jealousies – that I really wanted to do something 'big' now.

The training session was hardly enough. I had set my sights on a mountain and I needed to prepare myself adequately for it. I had to do something. One night, as everyone around me slept, I decided to take the risk of walking all by myself. I also knew that I couldn't afford to fall. For if I fell and injured myself while attempting to walk that would be the end of my dream of scaling the Everest. I uttered a small prayer and then, resting my hands on the edge of the bed, I gingerly placed my right leg on the ground. The touch of earth was strange. I quickly decided that I would walk wall to wall. This way, I would be able to walk without risking a fall.

Hurray! I was walking . . . walking on my own . . . without anyone around me. I felt as if I was flying in the air. I was overjoyed. Without me noticing it, several pairs of eyes were busy recording my 'activity'. I hadn't realized that CCTVs were placed all around the ward.

Unlike CCTVs at railway stations that are mostly non-functional, the ones here were working fine. Next morning a delegation of doctors, including the AIIMS director, visited me to advise me against walking alone. They warned me about the perils and pitfalls of my actions. They also had the artificial leg removed at night to ensure that I didn't defy the orders. But walking alone had done my confidence a world of good. I had tasted blood. Despite being warned I was dying to walk again, all by myself. Next day, I spoke to the AIIMS director and his team. I told them that I felt fit enough to walk by myself and proceeded to give a brief demonstration to them that I was indeed safe and supremely confident even while walking alone.

They said it takes nearly a year for people to get accustomed to an artificial limb. But I told them that unlike other patients who take their time to recover, I had a 'mission' to accomplish. I didn't reveal the actual goal I had set my eyes on for I knew that they would, after hearing my plans, take me to be mentally unstable. Without revealing the complete truth, I just persisted with my pleas. I must have sounded convincing enough. The look on the faces of the doctors communicated the fact that they were finding it hard to believe how, after just a couple of days of training, someone could walk so effortlessly on a 'foreign' leg. Reluctantly, they nodded after a quick consultation. I was warned against getting too adventurous and told that my request would be only partially granted. I was allowed to walk alone but under supervision. I agreed. The more I walked, the more confident I became. In fact, I felt liberated.

IN JULY, FOUR MONTHS AFTER I WAS WHEELED INTO this much-in-demand hospital, I was finally free from hospital bondage. I had spent much time in this famous hospital, mainly undergoing surgical procedures and post-operative care. I could only get to walk towards the end of my stay at AIIMS, the training period lasting barely a couple of days. The AIIMS doctors had been startled to discover that I had learnt to walk with an artificial limb in a couple of days when many took a year or even more. Their astonishment had boosted my belief in my ability to carry out seemingly impossible tasks.

As I came out of the hospital, I saw the media and the ever-so-familiar cameras. The media had become like family. I smiled and waved at them. They returned the gesture and wished me well. They may have been driven by professional considerations while covering me yet, after my family, they were the ones who spent the most amount of time with me.

Hardly a day passed when I was not required to give a byte as I met them practically every day. Their faces changed as cities changed – Bareilly to Delhi via Lucknow – yet for me they were like one big joint family, united by a common purpose to get to the truth and force the authorities to initiate corrective action. There were occasions when I saw them going without food for hours just so that they could run a story on time.

I remember a journalist once telling me that he used to eat, drink and even sleep with his stories!

'WHY DO YOU WANT BACHENDRI PAL'S MOBILE NUMBER?'

The query had come from a woman journalist of CNN-IBN – a prominent news channel – which I had made the request to. She had come to interview me at the fifth-floor Kotla Mubarakpur guest house that Ajay Maken's aides had arranged for us. What surprised the woman journalist was me asking for the mountaineer's contact. A girl with an artificial left limb and a damaged right, with a steel rod inserted into it, was hardly expected to scout for a mountaineer. And Bachendri Pal has been India's most prominent woman mountaineer and the first from the country to scale Mt Everest.

Google her and you will discover how she has inspired several girls and women to take up mountaineering.

The problem was that her contact details were not available on the internet. Ever since I had made up my mind to scale the Everest, I desperately wanted to meet her. But how and where would I meet her? I had no idea where she lived. My problem was that I was a bit reluctant to ask it from anyone. The few people to whom I had confided my plans of scaling the Everest had described me as 'mad'. They thought that I had lost my mind.

Since then, I had started keeping my plans to myself. I would meet women who would express sympathy, bemoan my leg loss, feel sorry for me and wonder aloud about how I was going to spend the rest of my life. They would leave after telling me to 'Have faith in God. He will help you!' It was around this time that I met this journalist. I had just arrived at this guest house from AIIMS. We wondered how I would go up to the fifth floor as the guest house didn't have a lift.

I refused to be carried on a stretcher as my family and friends were suggesting. I told them that having set my sights on Mt Everest I would have to learn to climb these stairs on my own. I was still climbing the stairs when I got a call from this journalist wanting to interview me. I had earlier told her that I was going to shift to this guest house and that she could come directly there. The journalist had arrived and was calling to check if I was there. I told her that I was climbing up to the guest house and that she too would have to come by the stairs.

She carried out the thirty-minute interview and at the end, pleasantly surprised by my attitude, she said, 'Please feel free to ask for any help.' In life opportunity doesn't knock twice. You have to realize this and seize the moment. The offer made by the journalist gave me a ray of hope. Immediately I told her that if she wanted to help, she should get me the cell phone number of Bachendri Pal. When she asked why I wanted the number, I lied. 'I just want to meet her,' I said. The journalist promised to arrange for the number and left.

Now, the three of us – Rahul, Sahib and me – were all alone, thinking of ways to make 'Mission Everest' successful. Three hours later, I got a call from the journalist. She had managed to get Bachendri Pal's mobile phone number. We called Pal instantly. We called repeatedly for nearly five days but there was no response. On the sixth day, she answered the call. I introduced myself. She said she had heard about me and invited me to Jamshedpur. I hadn't told her the reason why I wanted to meet her. That was simply because I wanted to tell her of my 'Everest desire' in person rather than over the phone.

Stung by the accusations that were hurled at me, I was now more determined than ever before to prove myself. The country knew me as a victim. I wanted them to now know me as a winner. I had no idea if I would be successful in achieving my goal. But I was clear that even if I had to go down, I would do so with a fight. All our religious scriptures are full of such advice – to do one's karma and leave the rest to the Almighty.

My mind was now at peace. Having talked to Bachendri Pal, I felt elated. I had spoken to the first Indian woman to have scaled the Everest. But, before going to Jamshedpur there was something else to attend to as well. I wanted to go on a thanksgiving visit to Bareilly. It was there that I had met Pintu Kashyap and B.C. Yadav, the two people who had saved my life. It was in Bareilly that a poor woman had given her shawl to me as I lay by the track side, shivering in the cold. I wanted to do all this to encourage people to continue to help others in distress like me. So days after being discharged from AIIMS, I was on my way there.

The visit proved to be an eye opener. After visiting Chaneti, where I was thrown out of the Padmawat Express, I met Pintu Kashyap. He told me how the police, especially the GRP, was out to harass him simply because he had spoken on TV favourably about me. I was happy that I visited Bareilly, for people like Pintu didn't have anyone to fall back upon. I told them that I was with them. Sahib even spoke on TV criticizing the GRP's handling of the case and the manner in which it was targeting the poor for telling the truth. The GRP and its bosses had tried every trick in the book to frame me.

They knew that my case had put them in the dock as the issue of women's safety on trains was now in the spotlight. A thanksgiving trip was definitely called for and I was happy that I had come. I also met B.C. Yadav who was delighted to see me. He said he was happy that he gave blood to a good person. 'The fact that you have come to meet us shows that you are good at heart,' he said. Here, I also went to meet a delegation of deaf and dumb kids who had come to express their solidarity with me when I was lying in the Bareilly district hospital. They couldn't speak yet they conveyed their concern to me and cheered me up with their smiles and gestures. Their eyes spoke about the purity of their intention.

It was such an irony that these children garlanded me and offered me an award at a time when the railway cops were busy questioning my motives. I had been filled with a lot of positive energy when they had turned up at my bedside to cheer me up. Now they inspired me again with their warm welcome. I expressed my sincere thanks to them. They smiled, waved at me and left after blowing kisses at me. It was now time to leave. We took a train to Lucknow.

After spending a day, I decided to visit the K.D. Singh Babu Stadium. Here, word spread about my arrival. Among many others who came to see me train and talk to me were some journalists of the *Hindustan Times*. They saw me playing and clicked me in various poses.

My photographs were prominently carried on page one. This acted like an elixir – filling me up with confidence. Well begun is half done! Mission Everest was on course. Now, I became even more desperate to meet Bachendri Pal. My family again got ready to travel with me – this time to Jamshedpur. Since we were unable to locate a direct train, we boarded the early morning Gomti Express from Lucknow to New Delhi.

There we boarded the Purushottam Express to Jamshedpur in the bogie reserved for the handicapped. I was travelling with a normal ticket and had no idea about the norms to travel in this compartment. Just before the train was about to leave, some security staff entered the compartment and began checking if all the persons with disability were carrying a certificate with them. It was very strange that rather than noticing the disability, the security guys were keen on the paper proof of their handicap. I had a certificate from AIIMS stating that I was now a handicapped person. The security staff, however, refused to accept it. They only recognized a certificate from the district administration. Mine wasn't ready by then. I was rudely asked to vacate the compartment. I refused and got into an argument.

In a fit of extreme anger at their insensitive manner, I decided to show them that I wasn't faking my handicap. I took off my artificial limb and waved it at the security team. 'Look, here's the proof. I am not stepping down. Go and call your bosses if you still have doubts,' I said. The ticket-checking staff beat a hasty retreat. I actually followed them shouting, 'Look, this is the proof . . .'

But why should things come to this? Rules are meant to be followed but people should also apply reason. At least for such a clearly visible handicap like mine, people shouldn't be harassed just because they aren't carrying a piece of paper from the district administration. The certificate can lie at times. But eyes won't. I think the railway authorities need to pay attention to this aspect. Every day several people are probably facing such harassment. Any civilized society needs to ensure that this doesn't happen. I broke down in tears the moment the train left the station. The fact that I was now travelling in a compartment meant for handicapped people made me sad.

Tears welled up in my eyes as my mind raced back to that train journey I undertook on board the Padmawat Express – the one that ended at Chaneti near Bareilly. The harrowing events of the recent past flashed up before my eyes, more vivid than the present. I felt weak and emotional and fell asleep soon after. Next morning we were at Jamshedpur. We called up Bachendri Pal. 'Madam, we have arrived at the station.' The country's first woman mountaineer thought we were calling her up from the Delhi railway station to inform her that we were about to start for Jamshedpur. 'Madam, we are at the Jamshedpur railway station.' Bachendri Pal sounded genuinely surprised. She had not thought that I was so anxious and committed to meet her. 'Oh! Good, good. In that case, wait there please. I will send my car to fetch you.' I politely declined her offer. 'Madam, you just tell us where to reach. We will be there.'

After we had the address, we hired an auto whose driver helped us locate Bachendri Pal's office. I had to climb some stairs to reach her office which I did holding Sahib's hand as I was yet to fully familiarize myself with the artificial limb. There were blisters and boils all over both my legs along with several stitches on my right leg which also had a rod inserted into it. Bachendri Pal cried aloud after watching me climb up and the state of my legs. After a while she asked me what had brought me to her. So far I had merely said that I wanted to meet her as I felt inspired by her. That was basically to keep in check sceptical looks from coming my way. Now, for the first time I told her my plan. 'Madam, I want to try climbing the mountain that you scaled long back.'

If she was surprised, she didn't make it that obvious. Instead she smiled. She was more encouraging than I could have imagined, telling me that I was a brave girl and that scaling a mountain as one's goal after what I had been through was surely praiseworthy. While speaking to me, she suddenly paused, thought awhile and took out her mobile phone which she used to call up the journalists of the *Telegraph* and the *Times of India*. Since the mountain lady is much respected and widely admired, journalists take her seriously. It showed in the way representatives of such prominent papers turned up to meet her at such short notice.

When they arrived, Bachendri Pal showered praises on me. 'Look, she is thinking of scaling the Everest even in such a situation. Isn't it a classic example of a never-say-die approach?' The journalists nodded. Then turning towards me, she made a comment that I remember even today. 'In your heart you have already climbed the Everest. Now you merely need to prove it to the world!' After the journalists left, Bachendri Pal told me, 'Listen, child, I have my full sympathies with you. But the Everest is a tough ask. This is not to discourage you but to make you weigh the pros and cons of the decision you have made.' I knew why Bachendri Pal was saying so. It was normal too. After all, who would think that a female amputee could hold her own against the Everest? I told her to give me a chance to prove myself. She agreed.

'Join our Tata Steel Adventure Foundation at Uttarkashi. My staff will train you. We will see how you fare after which we can take a final call. As I said, you have already conquered the Everest in your heart. Now you just need to prove it to the world. Even otherwise, you are a winner for me. Good luck!'

MY LAST SEMESTER LAW EXAMINATION WAS DUE just about the time I reached Lucknow. I took the examination as I have always believed in the importance of education, especially for women. So many girls in UP, as indeed the rest of the country, are forced to miss out on studies due to the archaic belief that while boys should study to earn, girls should learn household chores so that they turn out to be good housewives. Our studies too smack of gender bias. Chapters taught in primary classes are full of narratives like 'Ram goes to school, Laxmi works in the kitchen' which strengthen gender stereotypes.

Women in our villages are still just considered vegetable makers and baby producers, playing the dutiful wife, the good sister, the obedient daughter. Boys can stay out late but girls have to be in before sunset.

Boys can dress up just as they want. For girls everyone wants a dress code. For boys it's cool to pass a comment on a girl but for us it's taboo. Now, women are here, there and of course, everywhere. They are driving taxis and trains, they are setting foot on the moon and going into space, they are in the armed forces and they are in politics. There are women boxers, athletes, cricketers and gymnasts. Women are making a mark as painters, authors, film-makers.

Still women are considered second to men. That hurts. This should change and for this women would have to learn to be bold. I am advocating not bra-burning feminism but the need to get girls to make educated and informed choices. This change can come only through education. I hardly had any time to prepare for the law papers. Still, I was satisfied with my performance.

I spent some time in Lucknow, resting my body before the mountain adventure I was about to set out on. Apart from Sahib and Rahul, no one was willing to take me seriously. But by now I had learnt to laugh such cynicism away. Apart from the two family members, I also got encouragement from Bachendri Pal as well as the media who was behind me all through. In fact, at one point the media was even blamed for highlighting me needlessly and creating hype merely to gain TRPs.

I wanted to answer such criticism by doing something big enough not just to silence my critics but to set at rest my own doubts about my ability. My doubts had surfaced after I was bombarded in the press with those lies. Even though I knew that it was part of a deep-rooted conspiracy to malign me, I couldn't completely get over the trauma of that attack. I had always been a positive person, a fighter. But could I really overcome the odds this time? While I smiled and acted positive, I didn't always believe it. Ultimately I wanted to climb the Everest to believe in myself again.

After about a month, we set out for Uttarkashi where Bachendri Pal had set up her makeshift training institute. On 28 February 2012, almost a year after I was pushed out of the train, we reached there. I called up Bachendri Pal to tell her that we had reached Uttarkashi. She was surprised again at how quickly I had reached. She asked someone in her team to bring me to the institute which was located 20 km away on the outskirts of the picturesque Sangam Chatti valley.

The institute was set up nearly 250 ft below on a rocky terrain. It was surrounded by peaks and located on the banks of the river Asi Ganga. Tata employees were given lessons in leadership and team spirit there. I was driven up to a particular point after which our luggage was unloaded and we were asked to walk 250 ft below along with luggage weighing 60 kg. In the hills such uneven spaces are created by nature. Here, it's fairly common to enter a third floor house from the top floor and then make your way down to the ground floor.

I was advised by locals to leave the luggage on the road itself and reach the camp first. Seeing the look of apprehension on my face, the locals laughed. They told me not to worry about the luggage. 'Don't worry. People here are God-fearing. In any case one wants to travel as light as possible in the hills. Even if one were to think of stealing this heavy luggage, one won't be able to go far with it,' a local said. Not for nothing are these hills also known as the abode of the gods.

Holding Sahib's hand I gradually made my way down to the camp, sliding and crawling most of the way. Sahib ensured that I reached there safely and then went up again to fetch the luggage. I was allotted a tent near the river to live. Sahib, who was used to living in such conditions during his stint with the paramilitary force, quickly created a small drain around the camp. That was done to ensure that neither rainwater nor reptiles like snakes entered the camp. Sahib was put up in an all-male tent. We had tea together.

Immediately afterwards, an instructor greeted us. 'I am Prateek Bhowmick,' he said and invited me out. Bhowmick examined and checked the status of both my legs. 'All right then, your training begins now,' he said in a typically military fashion and directed me to walk up the 250-ft-high path from which I had come down! 'What?' I was aghast at the idea of climbing all the way up all over again. But Bhowmick seemed to be in no mood to relent. Grudgingly I prepared for the climb. I knew going all the way up alone would be impossible. So I again requested Sahib to accompany me. In a little over two hours I had climbed 250 ft up and returned. Next morning we were asked to cover twice the area. I did that too.

The same evening another instructor visited us. He told us that I would have to join a group that was all set to go on a trek. Next day we were ready for our first trek ever. The group was to start a day later but we were asked to set out a day earlier due to my handicap. 'We will make our halt after 9 km. Since you have a handicap, I suggest you begin a day early,' he told me. Along with Sahib and a female assistant we set out on the route that was explained to us on paper. Sahib had served in the CISF for fifteen years. So he was well trained on these routes. I just followed him. Each step was like a big effort. Every time I exerted myself, the pressure on my artificial limb created a gash at the place from where my leg had been amputated. I kept on braving the pain but after nearly 2.5 km I broke down just ahead of a very steep climb.

On the mountains such emotional breakdowns are quite frequent. What I desperately needed was something to pump me up; some words of encouragement. Luckily Sahib was around to play that role. He told me that for someone who wants to scale Mt Everest, such hurdles should not mean much. Such encouragement provided the necessary kick. I shed my fear and agreed. After resting for a while I climbed another 3 km by the evening to reach a village. The head of this village agreed to put me up in his house along with a woman instructor. Sahib got to sleep in a barn.

The next morning we again set out on our next mission. My able-bodied team members hadn't reached the venue when we touched the 9-km goal by the evening. Sahib put up a tent. Two hours later the entire team reached us. They were surprised to find that we had reached the place – our first goal – successfully. In the evening, one of the course in-charges arrived and discussed with me and Sahib the route which we were to take on our return. 'Others will take a different route. I advise you to take the same route back,' he said.

He said that while the rest of the group were fully capable of taking the tougher route, I should return using the safer, old route. I put my foot down. 'No, I will also go by the same route you will use. At the most I am going to be left behind. But I won't change my mind.' The rest of the team was supposed to leave at 8 a.m. We decided to leave at 4 a.m. without even the woman assistant who said she was uncomfortable with my slow speed. In a way, she had refused to help me on a route she knew was much tougher than the one we had taken to reach here.

The assistant was very weak. I thought that she would not be able to lift me if required as her body weight was less than mine. In fact, that's what she confessed to me some months later. 'I am sorry that I left you all by yourself. But the fact was that I was scared. Since you had chosen to travel by the difficult route I knew that my task would be even more difficult,' she said. Now I had only Sahib to fall back on. Having taken a decision I decided to proceed ahead. By 6 a.m. we had reached a point which was considered dangerous. There were wild animals in the area and the terrain was very rocky. What's worse, there had been a recent landslide. We were now supposed to cross it. Our instructor had actually asked us to wait at this point. But having come this far, we were in no mood to stop. Both of us wanted to move ahead.

Sahib told me that he would first test the route before taking me along. After nearly ninety minutes, he returned and told me that though the route was indeed very risky, if others could cross it, so could I. 'We are going all by ourselves,' he declared. I nodded. Sahib took my bag and began crossing the dangerous stretch. We used ropes and mountain equipment to cross. By 10 a.m. we had successfully managed to cross the 1-km route. Now confident of our ability to make it even further, we decided to cover the entire stretch all by ourselves.

They didn't help us in this difficult phase so we must travel on our own now. This is a good chance for us to test the wild, we told ourselves. We moved ahead, losing our way at times. Having watched Discovery channel and mountain movies, we had some idea that when in doubt one should follow a river. So we simply followed the Asi Ganga and walking along its banks we finally reached the base camp at Sangam Chatti. There was chaos at the base camp. A rescue team was about to be sent for us as we had been 'missing' for a long time. The concern was genuine.

As we later discovered, other able members of the team had skipped the route that we had chosen just because it was way too dangerous. In fact those team members who had skipped the dangerous route had earlier spent a lot of time explaining to me why I shouldn't travel through the area and why they should. Naturally, we had taken more time in covering it. Everyone at the camp was astonished to hear that we had succeeded and the handicapped girl's determination spread like wildfire in the base camp.

Even Bachendri Pal was informed that I had overcome obstacles in a route that other team members had found difficult to cross. After the experience, my confidence skyrocketed. Indeed, a strong-willed person can overcome anything. Nothing can stop a truly determined soul. Bachendri Pal, who always pumped in fresh confidence in me, later told me: 'Arunima, you are far better than them. In fact these people now seem to be suffering from a handicap, not you. I am proud of you.'

I was delighted. My legs, however, were in bad shape. There were blisters on them and they hurt. But the sensation of victory had dimmed the intensity of the pain. I was as delighted and contented as an athlete who forgets the tiring grind after winning the Olympic medal, the manner in which a student forgets those sleepless nights spent learning complex equations and exults after answering all the questions correctly, the sheer joy with which a farmer wipes his sweat away on seeing the crop ready. For two days I continued to bask in the glory of my achievement. Now supremely confident, we decided to set out on our own. Though we still trailed other climbers by some margin, we were now pretty sure of bridging the gap.

We started spending more and more time on the mountains. Nothing seemed to matter now. I felt like I had been possessed by a strange beguiling dream of being on top of the world. And for that to happen I had to overcome barriers, challenge myself, push my body to the limit. The only thing that drove me now was preparing well enough for the final frontier. Poor, inexperienced mountaineers like us cannot match normal, moneyed mountain enthusiasts in resources. We have to manage on our limited stock, something we have been doing all our lives. We continued to train hard.

One day during training I encountered a steep climb. Sahib and I hadn't eaten anything. The team had left us and there was heavy snowfall too, to compound our problems. We lost our way. Tears welled up in my eyes. I was tired, hungry and frightened too. At this point Sahib said something that brought a smile on my lips. 'Neither your father nor mine has left anything for us. Our mission is the Everest. We have lost our way temporarily. But we will find it. The important thing is that we should not lose track of our mission.' Sahib then fetched some wood to light a fire and cook some Maggi. I felt refreshed. And once again we set out on our way. Soon we reached our destination. I had spent nearly two months in the mountains. I was now learning to use ropes to climb.

I didn't even need Sahib's helping hands to hold me as I climbed. I gradually discovered that the journey downhill was tougher than the climb. I was also required to carry 5 kg weight that was increased to 10 kg and even 20 kg as time wore on. I was doing well but it used to hurt me that though I was leaving base camp earlier than the regular trainees, they were frequently overtaking me. I asked myself whether I would ever be able to realize the mountain dream if I continued to trail others in this fashion.

I told myself that I needed to improve on my timing. It was true that I suffered from a handicap but then I wasn't here to gain sympathy. I was here to accomplish a mission. The mountain treats everyone equally. Only the truly committed pass the challenges that come one's way here. I kept motivating myself with such thoughts. It helped. It took me some months to improve my timing but I kept on trying without losing hope. Every day, I would try and set newer goals for myself – each more difficult than the other. At times it was frustrating, at times boring. But I kept trying. Slowly, the dedication bore fruit.

I started catching up with others. What's more, no one was overtaking me any more. And this clearly meant that I had started reaching our point earlier than them. When I started doing that quite regularly, the normal trainees started asking me what I ate! Such questions made me realize that I was getting better than them and in other words gearing up to realize my dream. Bachendri Pal arrived at the institute to camp a few days later. One of the reasons why she had come here was to check if I was indeed training or simply whiling away time.

In order to test how serious I was about the Everest, Bachendri Pal also started accompanying me on our usual treks. Every day she took us on a new route. When she saw that I was successfully doing whatever I was being asked to do, she said, 'Arunima, you have learnt 40 per cent of what a mountaineer should know. Now, I want you to do a basic mountaineering course. That is the first step for a professional mountaineer.'

I knew she was right. Having spent some time in the mountains had made me realize that even a little slip could prove costly. So following Pal's instructions, I visited the Nehru Institute of Mountaineering (NIM), also in Uttarkashi. Here we were shocked to discover that NIM doesn't admit handicapped people. The principal said they have never trained a handicapped person and cited rules that prohibit them from training people with disability.

But we were in no mood to give up. Sahib spoke to the principal, instructor and doctors of the institute and tried to convince them that it was as much in their interest as ours that I be trained. He threw the bait. 'Don't you want a world record to be made? Imagine a girl trained at your institute going on to make a record. It will bring such a good name to NIM.' The move worked. The NIM principal reluctantly agreed. But the doctor was still adamant. He refused to give a 'safe I' certificate, a must for taking the training. 'In case something happens, who will be responsible?' the doctor asked when we persisted.

I told him, 'Sir, mountains will come ten days later. Please watch me till then and give a clearance if you are satisfied with my progress.' The NIM people had also done a fact check on me. So finally it was agreed that before I took to the mountains I would have to undergo a ten-day training and only after completing it successfully would I be eligible for the 'safe I' certificate. I wasted no time in enrolling myself with NIM. From the next day my basic training course began. I had seventy-five girls from India and abroad for company. Of them I was the only handicapped girl.

I was treated like a normal person during the

training period and there was no one to assist me. An amusing incident took place one day. Our trainers had put up all the girls in groups of five to eight. The girls in my group belonged to different states like Delhi, Maharashtra and Uttarakhand. I was the only one from UP. Despite hailing from different states, we soon became good friends. Every day I was required to walk a 10-km stretch from the institute to Tekla, the rock climbing area, where I was trained in the art of mountain climbing. I was also required to carry heavy mountaineering equipment – including a 40 m 9 mm rope – weighing nearly 20 kg – till the training area. The girls in my group used to take good care of me. I still remember how a girl from America called Deeya Suzannah Bajaj used to go out of her way to help me.

One day while I was on my way to Tekla, the screw of my artificial limb came loose. This resulted in me falling down. The girls in my group came to my rescue and tried to lift me up. As they did so, the stump slipped off. The girls got scared by the sight and dropped me in reflex. I fell down all over again. I could see how frightened the girls were at the sight of my stump. So I told them to stay calm even as I got busy tightening the screws of my artificial leg. Soon I was ready to walk again. On the way to Tekla all of us had a big laugh about how the group had become scared of my artificial leg.

I approached each day with new zeal. After ten days of intense and gruelling training the NIM doctor agreed to give me a 'safe I'. We started from Bhukkhi Road and headed towards a place called Tel in the mountains. It was a very testing climb. It helped that all the five girls in my group had become good friends. I was given the honour of leading my group. Unlike the girls in other groups who didn't seem as enthusiastic, our group was quite energetic and high on enthusiasm. The five of us were the cynosure of all eyes as our chemistry and timing were the best among all the seventy-five girls.

In fact we were often tasked with motivating the girls in other groups. We pushed them to move until, irritated, they would beg us to leave them alone. There was one girl called Madhuwanti Godse. She was a bit plump and hence moved slowly. Whenever I egged her on to move quickly, she used to say with a smile, 'Arunima, who would say that you are handicapped? You are able to do it with just one leg what we are unable to do with both.'

By now we had reached the base camp which was full of beautiful flowers. We wanted to spend time there, to pluck flowers and put them in our hair. But a mountaineer is supposed to be disciplined. So instead of plucking the flowers, we merely enjoyed seeing them. All five of us were put up in a common tent there. We were really having fun in each other's company but we were also learning how to survive in the mountains. We remained at the base camp for two days after which we had to leave for the main summit at 18,000 ft. On a cloudy day we did the summit. We embraced each other in excitement and took a selfie. By 7 p.m. the same day we were back at the base camp. Our group was the first to do the summit.

The moment I reached the base camp, Digambar, the main instructor of the group, informed me that I had to rush for a job interview at the CISF headquarters in Delhi. 'You are required to be there day after tomorrow,' the instructor said. The job interview was for the post of a CISF head constable. The interview had come about primarily due to the efforts of Nirmaljeet Singh Kalsi, a joint secretary in the Ministry of Home Affairs who had visited me at AIIMS. After I was discharged, I paid a courtesy call to him at his North Block office. The officer again offered help. At this we told him that I had lost out on an opportunity to get a job in the CISF for no fault of mine. Had I not been thrown out of the Delhi-bound train, I would perhaps have become a head constable by now. So I told the officer that it would be great if he could do something to revive that job offer. Kalsi promised to do something and he kept his word.

My training was over but the CISF deadline was too close. I had to travel down from a height of 16,000 ft, roughly 29 km, in a day – a distance that people usually cover in five days. And I still had to take a written test the next day. Meanwhile, Sahib told me through a satellite phone from Uttarkashi that he had sent an e-mail to the CISF people requesting that the deadline be extended. It was expected that the CISF would consider the request. However, there had not been any return mail confirming that the interview had been rescheduled.

I wanted to test myself under all conditions and at all costs. So I decided to try and cover the distance of 29 km in a day. At 6 a.m. I started climbing down and by 4 p.m. I reached Bhukkhi Road. Many thought this was an eye-popping achievement. I still meet mountaineers who need convincing that I actually travelled down 16,000 ft (29 km) in a day. At Bhukkhi I found Sahib waiting for me with a taxi. Without wasting any time we set out for Haridwar that very night.

Travel on this route at night to Haridwar or Dehradun isn't encouraged. We were stopped at several places and had to explain the purpose for travelling at night before we were allowed to proceed. At 2 a.m. we reached the Rishikesh bus station and not wanting to waste any more time we set out immediately for Delhi. Travelling constantly through the night, we reached the CISF HQ at Delhi at 9 a.m. Bless my leg – I had now travelled a record twenty-seven hours non-stop to reach Delhi!

The DIG, CISF was surprised to see me. That was because he was told barely twenty-seven hours back that I was deep in the mountains of Uttarkashi. The CISF official had been a mountaineer himself and hence found it difficult to believe me. To confirm our version, he even spoke to the NIM principal. After the confirmation the CISF official appeared really impressed. The official had already agreed to Sahib's request on the mail to postpone the interview by a week. I had no option but to return.

We took a bus from Delhi at around 10 a.m. to reach Rishikesh by 6 p.m. the same day. From there we hired a taxi to Uttarkashi, reaching NIM by 3 a.m. That morning I took the written test that I had failed to take earlier. I was surprised to discover that the team of able men and women who had climbed 16,000 ft had not come back still, while I had returned from Delhi by that time!

The principal told me that the team would return after two hours. The next day I participated in the training ceremony and headed for the Tata Steel Adventure Foundation. There I began my normal schedule – climbing up and coming down. I trained for another month. On Bachendri Pal's advice, I even travelled to Gaumukh (or Gomukh) – the point where the Ganga originates.

That was a fascinating journey. Along with our guide we set out for the place at 4 a.m. and reached Gangotri at 2 p.m. Having travelled non-stop we wanted to get some rest but the guide wanted us to keep moving. We weren't happy with the way the guide was trying to set the terms. But, in the mountains, the guide is the boss.

It's wise to listen to him. So, unmindful of the blisters and pain, I kept walking till we reached Chir Basa. It was 7 p.m. We still had to cover another 6 km before the base camp at Bhoj Basa – where we were supposed to make a halt.

Now even the guide agreed to break journey at this point. He, however, announced that there were no facilities at Chir Basa. We were struggling to find a place to spend the night when a forest sub-inspector informed us that a moody, mystic saint called Nangu Baba who lived nearby along the banks of the Ganga could offer us some shelter. 'He is a mysterious sadhu. If you are lucky he may allow you to spend the night in his cave where he has made some basic arrangements.' Locating the saint wasn't difficult. Nangu Baba met us warmly. 'Arunima, I have nothing to give to you. You can live in this cave if you want and I will make some chapattis for you with the little flour I have left.' He cooked six chapattis for the three of us and served them with jaggery (gur). There was something divine about the saint. Even the simple chapattis he had cooked for us tasted brilliant! After dinner we made ourselves as comfortable as we could in the dark cave. Outside the weather had turned really bad. The skies opened up, and soon there was heavy snowfall which added to the chill. In the background, the holy Ganges started making loud, scary noises.

We called out to Nangu Baba who was nowhere to be seen. Though we called out his name several times, there was no answer. Cold and fear kept us awake through the night.

We set out for Bhoj Basa early in the morning, at about 4 a.m. As we were walking away, our attention was drawn towards someone reciting Lord Shiva's name. That was Nangu Baba, chanting the mantra of *Om Namah Shivay* while bathing in the near-freezing temperature in the river. We were covered from head to toe in woollens but the chill didn't seem to have any impact on the mountain saint. I walked towards him and sought permission to leave. The Baba smiled and said, 'Okay. Meet me on your return.'

We now walked continuously for seven hours to cover a distance of 6 km and reached Bhoj Basa by 11 a.m. Our next destination was Gaumukh which was a little over 4 km from there. Again the guide turned down our request for taking some rest. The weather wasn't very good. So we thought it might be safe to move the next day. But the guide rudely told us that we couldn't rest and had to move on. He was like an army official not wanting to take no for an answer. Like loyal troops we set out for Gaumukh after leaving our belongings with another mountain saint, Lal Baba, who is the head priest of a temple at Bhoj Basa.

Walking continuously we reached Gaumukh at 4 p.m., where I was stunned by the breathtaking sight. The glaciers seemed to beckon to me; and I walked towards them unmindful of the dangers ahead. By the time my guide and Sahib saw me, I had already walked right till the edge of the glacier. I wanted to get as close to the point of the Ganga's origin as possible. In fact I was feeling a strange pull, as if some divine force was pushing me to move and to become one with nature. From behind me I could hear the guide and Sahib shout, asking me to return immediately.

We were the only people around as trekking time had ended. 'Please turn back, please don't go ahead,' they called out to me. I now realized the danger and slowly turned back. Almost as soon as I stepped back, the glacier on which I had stood crumbled and fell nearly 500 ft below. Had I stayed on the glacier even for a second more, I would have met an icy end. The guide and Sahib were livid. I apologized. 'I wanted to check if the place from where the Ganga originates is actually like a cow's mouth,' I told them. Gaumukh: *gau* – cow and *mukh* – mouth.

The weather had turned bad again. Heavy snowfall started. There was no place available for shelter. Even as we were wondering what to do, icy winds arrived. Our guide, who was in an unusually bad mood throughout the trip, now started fearing for his life and fled. Once again Sahib and I were left all alone to fend for ourselves. We survived somehow by taking shelter below an overhead rocky arch. After an hour or so, as the snowfall slowed down a bit, we decided to leave. But the problem was that the entire area was now covered with a thick layer of snow. This meant that tracing the return route would be nearly impossible now as our footprints had been buried beneath the snow. On one side there was the mountain and on the other side there was the free-flowing Ganges.

Fortunately, at this point we saw some mountain goats. We decided to follow them, thinking that they would lead us somewhere, most probably to a village. It turned out to be a wise move. Following them we managed to trace our way back. By the time we reached Bhoj Basa, it was 11 p.m. and I was in really bad shape.

We arrived at Lal Baba's place where we also found the guide who had deserted us. After coming to know what the guide had done, Lal Baba gave him a piece of his mind. He then made us stay with him and offered us food. We spent the night at his temple. At 6 a.m. the next day he told us that we could leave. We reached Gangotri at 5 p.m. From there we took a taxi to the Tata Steel Adventure Foundation.

The next day we met Bachendri Pal and briefed her about our trip to Gaumukh and how I had nearly died. The ace mountaineer heard us patiently. After I finished she pointed out the flaws – not carrying a 'headlight', for instance. 'If you had carried it, you could have kept moving and would not have had to put up with Nangu Baba,' she said. She was right. One of the reasons – apart from being tired – why we had taken shelter in Baba's cave was that we couldn't see anything in the night. Bachendri Pal also told us the virtue of patience, which she said was one of the key features of a mountaineer. 'Patience and ability to acclimatize to all kinds of situations and to listen to the guide at all times is the key,' she said.

I nodded. Sahib spoke to Bachendri Pal in the evening: 'Ma'am, now Arunima has successfully completed all the tasks you had set for her. She is ready for Mt Everest.' But Bachendri Pal still had her doubts. She suggested that we should wait till 2014 or 2015. At this, Sahib firmly told her that our deadline was 2013. Bachendri Pal realized we were set on our plan. So she agreed. However, she had a condition. She said that, before Everest, I would have to prove myself by scaling Chamsar Kangdi in Ladakh on the China–Tibet border. 'If you climb this 21,798-foot mountain successfully you will be on your way to the Everest,' she told us.

We agreed and immediately set out to our new destination – Ladakh. Travelling three days at a stretch we reached Karjok, the last Indian village before the China–Tibet border. From Karjok the Chinese border is barely 40 km away. After Karjok, it's virtually no man's land. There are army posts but no civilians. Our team had twenty-one people and the base camp was situated at 18,000 ft. By the time we reached the base camp, sixteen of the nineteen members in the party had retired. Sahib himself brought several people down from 20,000 feet, one of them being Bachendri Pal's elder brother. However, along with Bachendri Pal's other brother Rajendra Pal, who is a supremely fit mountaineer, and two others, I continued to move up . . . up and up to ultimately reach the top and hoist the national flag.

Bachendri Pal who had arrived at the base camp by now had lovingly prepared aloo parathas for us, which she brought for us till 20,000 feet, where we had set up the upper base camp. I enjoyed the parathas at the cold altitude but I wasn't able to meet Bachendri Pal as it had turned very dark by the time we arrived at the upper base camp. Bachendri Pal had left for the base camp by then. We spent the night at the upper base camp and the next day, Bachendri Pal greeted me at the base camp. '*Meri sherni* (my lioness),' she said and took me in her warm embrace. We now came down to the transit camp where Bachendri Pal's elder brother, who had fallen ill on the way to the top, was undergoing treatment.

In the evening, Bachendri Pal announced that I was finally ready for the Everest. She also assured me that she would talk to the officials at Tata Steel and that she was hopeful that I may get them to sponsor my Everest dream. Her clearance meant a lot to me. In fact, till such time as Bachendri Pal gave me the green light, I had my doubts about the Everest plan. I knew that her knowledge of the Everest was second to none. Her advice meant all the more to me for she was a woman and was perhaps better placed to address my concerns than anyone else. 'Never forget that on the mountains you can't take anything for granted,' Pal told me. I listened to her very carefully. So far her advice had stood me in good stead.

I still remember that day when, during my training at Uttarkashi, we encountered wild monkeys in November. We had gone out to collect wood to light a fire to keep the tent warm. As we were busy collecting wood from a dead tree, the wild monkeys ransacked our tent. They tore our clothes and damaged whatever they could lay their hands on.

We were left with nothing, literally nothing. To make things worse, heavy snowfall began just as we started moving towards the nearest village in search of food and shelter. We were stranded. We had no option but to wait for the snowfall to end. It went on all night. The snowfall finally stopped in the morning and by that time the entire area was covered in snow, making it impossible for us to retrace our steps. We forgot the route and wandered into the jungles and were ultimately forced to take shelter in a cave. Hungry and thirsty, we discovered some traces of water inside the cave. Tracing its origin, we reached the point from where water was trickling in tiny drops from inside the cave. In nearly thirty minutes we collected 200 ml of water. We also melted some hard ice that we found inside.

But we desperately needed something to eat. Lodged in a cave we were running out of ideas, when I suddenly remembered that Pal had taught me what to do if ever I was stuck in such a situation. She had taught me how to identify mountain plants that were edible and provided energy too. I decided to hunt for such plants in the cave and soon spotted some. Here it's important to emphasize that, if one does not have a good knowledge of such plants, one should never indulge in any guesswork. A wrong choice could cause more harm than good.

The plant that we ate is known as *lingdi.* In its infancy, it has miraculous properties. But as it grows, it turns poisonous and is then known as deadly grass (*bicchu ghaas*). The Himalayas is also home to *yarsagumba* (*Ophiocordyceps sinensis*), a sort of Himalayan bat-moth caterpillar which is invaded by a fungus and is famous for its medicinal properties. It's usually found in Himalayan ranges above 3500 m and is considered a powerful aphrodisiac not only in India but in countries like China where it is in huge demand. Many travel annually to these hills in search of a magical caterpillar lookalike, a kilogram of which can fetch a fortune in the international market.

Meanwhile, after staying in the same cave for three days during which we survived on lingdi, we finally found our way to the nearest village where a kind villager offered us shelter. He had barely enough to make ends meet but still he offered us rice. We had rice and salt here. On the fourth day we managed to reach the base camp located at a height of 15,000 ft. On yet another occasion, while on the way to a base camp on a different route at 16,500 ft at Darwa pass, we encountered heavy snowfall. The entire route was covered with snow. It was February. Sahib and I were moving on this route along with a cook and one Annu Madam who was our instructor. Annu Madam was constantly telling me to keep towards the mountains and not towards the cliff.

However, at one point I disobeyed her advice and started walking towards the cliff-side where I slipped and lost my balance. I remember Pal had once told me to thank God for everything. Truly enough if ever

I had to thank the Almighty for bestowing me with a handicap, it was this moment as my artificial leg got stuck in the soft ice. That saved me because that stopped my slide down. Annu Madam was in front of me and Sahib and a porter – he was returning from a point and had joined us – were behind. The porter dived in front to catch me by my hair while Annu Madam held on to my leg. Sahib held on to my hand but, as he pulled me, he too started sliding.

Somehow I survived and promised to behave. I knew how close I had been to meeting my end. For me that porter was a godsend, without whose help I surely wouldn't have survived. Meanwhile I again returned to Uttarkashi to continue my training. I was doing this to ensure that there was no dip in my fitness levels. I continued to train and practise in the mountains even in December–January, when Tata Steel Adventure closes down. We trained for the whole of February and till 15 March 2013, after which I got a call from Bachendri Pal who was in Jamshedpur now.

She called to tell me to reach Delhi by 25 March. I knew the big moment had arrived and immediately left the Uttarakhand hills for Lucknow where I met my relatives and, after about a week's stay, headed for

Delhi. I also visited the Vaishno Devi temple in Jammu, taking the stairs to reach the holy shrine in four hours' time. The CRPF which guards the shrine arranged for a special darshan for me. After seeking the blessings of the goddess – I prayed that if my Everest visit was successful I would visit her again – I again took the stairs on my way down.

From here we took a train to Lucknow. After reaching the state capital we wasted no time in setting out for the national capital where I was to answer a nation wanting to know if I would be able to do it.

THE PRESS WAS WAITING FOR ME AT THE DELHI Press Club.

I was used to the media but this gathering – a mix of Indian and foreign journalists – resembled one usually reserved for celebrities and top politicians. Sporting a nervous smile and feeling a touch edgy, I walked inside the hall longing for the two women who were closest to me – my mother and my elder sister. I didn't have enough funds to fly them here and it would have been unimaginable for them to blow their little savings away on an air trip.

I would start on my Everest expedition directly after the press meet – who knew if I would be able to see them again. Bachendri Pal perhaps understood the emotional turmoil I was undergoing. So she became extra supportive, cheering and encouraging me all through. Having gone out of her way to train and brief me on the various moods of the mountain, she again cautioned me against becoming overconfident.

'Even a little mistake can be deadly. Up there, there's no second chance,' she said.

Representing family was my brother Rahul who had come from Lucknow with *gujiya*, biscuits and laddoos – all made by him. Since my mother and sister weren't able to come, he thought home-cooked food would cheer me up. For a girl, all these things matter a lot. My brother won me over with his emotional gesture.

I was on a strict diet plan but, unable to resist the temptation to test my brother's culinary skills, I tasted some of the goodies he had prepared. They were delicious!

That made me wonder why the kitchen is always associated with women. Men can cook just as well. There are so many famous male chefs and I think it's time we do away with gender stereotypes. There are many husbands who would love to cook for their wives and family but don't due to old-fashioned ideas that women are supposed to cook while men earn. Unless we change our mindsets, all this talk of women empowerment that we keep hearing will remain a sham.

My mother and sister may not have been able to be present but luckily for me, other friends were at the Press Club that day. There were Baba Jagdeo Prasad (a resident of Banthara locality in Lucknow, he had become a grandpa to me), Raj Kishore (someone who called me his sister and played the genial banker) – both of whom had provided me an interest-free loan to partially fund the cost of a spare artificial limb – and, of course, the ever-reliable Sahib. How patient my sister had been to let him go for these fourteen months of training – without Sahib, I wouldn't have been able to be here. These three wonderful men, along with Rahul, were to accompany me to Kathmandu from where I would begin my climb.

Seeing their faces in the middle of a sea of strangers reminded me of many others who had helped me get this far. There was Swami Nikhileshwaranandji, the secretary of Swami Vivekananda Memorial Hall, Vadodara who had given me photographs of Swami Vivekananda, Ramakrishna Paramhansa and Maa Sharda Devi and had told me to have faith.

'You will get energy from them if you believe in them and in yourself,' he had said on coming to know about my Everest plan. He had called me a little ahead of the

Delhi press conference and offered help. 'Please let me know if you need something,' he had offered. At this, I had shared with him my biggest worry.

Despite taking a soft loan from people like Raj Kishore and others, I was still short of nearly Rs 70,000 for the spare limb. Swamiji promised help and he delivered by quickly raising the sum through donations. He was so prompt that by the time I arrived for the press meet, I had a spare limb with me.

There were others, two doctor-brothers – US-based Dr Rakesh and Delhi-based Dr Shailesh Srivastava. As a child Dr Rakesh was thrown off a moving train by a vendor selling his wares in the compartment. A train ran over his leg just like it had over mine. The incident didn't shatter him. Instead, he studied hard and, as luck would have it, became a doctor who specialized in artificial limbs.

He found a decent job in California and, with the help of his Delhi-based doctor-brother, developed a newer technique to provide a cheaper, lighter artificial limb to the needy in India through Innovative – the company launched jointly by the doctor duo. Dr Rakesh had learnt about my case after reading a report on the internet and immediately instructed

Dr Shailesh to get in touch with me. They got in touch with me at AIIMS to make the 'limb' offer. At that point several big companies were also anxious to donate a limb to me. However, the doctors at AIIMS and my family decided to go for the one being offered by these two wonderful brothers. Seeing the familiar faces gathered around me, and remembering the kindness of others, I felt both touched and grateful. The event was a blur of emotion. I don't quite remember what the media queries were like. There were several of them – about the mountain, its challenges, my handicap and stuff like that. Some media persons wanted to know if it was all a publicity-seeking exercise. They had every right to be cynical. No one thought I had a chance. I remember giving decent answers to the queries. After all, I was supposed to face the cameras confidently. A girl wanting to climb the Everest was expected to be brave. I have always believed that if you have to cry, you should do so alone. The world wants to see a winner; it mocks losers and those who break down.

When a journalist asked me how I was feeling, I told him with a smile that I was feeling great and that people with determination succeeded in overcoming the harshest of tests. But the whole time, there were butterflies inside my stomach. I was nervous, frightened and jittery. Even as I was making these grand statements I knew that the 'mountain deed' – assuming I was able to pull through – would eventually be my most credible response to my critics.

After the event, I went to shop for things I would require on those icy heights – clothes and other equipment. I also had a trident of Lord Shankar with me, which we had purchased a day after being discharged from AIIMS. Now, in Delhi I also bought a red cloth which I wrapped the trident with. Having purchased everything from the material to the spiritual, I was ready – ready for the mountain.

ON MY WAY TO THE AIRPORT, I SAW AN AEROPLANE ON the Delhi skyline. I had been inside an aeroplane only once before – but that was an air ambulance which was used to fly me from Lucknow to Delhi's AIIMS.

The sight momentarily transported me back to my childhood when I would get very excited on seeing planes fly above our house in Ambedkarnagar. Whenever I saw them, especially at night, I used to clap excitedly, saying: '*Chandrama uda ja raha hai* (the moon is flying)'. That's because I used to think the twinkling lights of aeroplanes were the moon itself. Now, of course I know that the moon doesn't fly.

I also know now that those planes which zoomed overhead creating a loud noise and left behind a trail of smoke across the sky were fighter planes while the low-noise ones that moved gracefully were passenger planes. Back then all planes appeared the same. Just watching them used to give me so much pleasure but never in my wildest dreams had I imagined that I would travel in them one day. To me the plane in the sky seemed to symbolize the burning human desire to give wings to one's dreams.

In a few hours from now I would be on another plane flying to Kathmandu. It would be a career-defining flight – one that would either ground me in life or let me soar high.

As my flight took off, I was once again reminded of my childhood expression: '*Chandrama uda ja raha hai . . .*'

All I wanted to do was to peep through the window to see how small the earth looks from above. Unfortunately I was in the middle seat and a foreigner was sitting by the window. But I couldn't resist leaning, every now and then, towards the window to catch an eye-full of the earth below. After two and a half hours we were hovering above Nepal's capital city of Kathmandu. For a first-timer, I was damn nervous as the flight descended. But thankfully the airline crew and Bachendri Pal, who was sitting right beside me, were there to help me remain calm.

After completing the post-landing formalities, we came out of the airport to be welcomed in traditional Nepalese style by the Asian Trekking agency that had been hired by the Tatas to take care of me.

They drove me to the Asian Trekking office where I was made to fill up an insurance form – each mountaineer who goes through an agency is insured – and was also briefed about the rules.

I was told not to insist on completing the summit if the guide or the Sherpa decided that the weather or other conditions weren't suitable. The message was clear – up there, the Sherpa is the boss. He takes decisions which the climber is supposed to follow. I was then introduced to my boss-to-be – short and stout Sherpa Neema Kancha, who was to accompany me to the summit and back. There was an artificial mountain wall in the office to give people a feel of a mountain. I saw many trying it out. Seeing others climb, I too decided to give it a try.

Seeing me climb the wall, my brother Rahul, who hadn't received any formal training at all, decided to give it a try. As he climbed the wall, everyone who had gathered there clapped. I felt nice.

Rahul later said that he drew inspiration from me.

'I am your brother. My failure would have embarrassed you since you have overcome extreme difficulties to succeed. So I had to win,' he said. I was slowly beginning to understand that everyone had high expectations from me. People had started believing in me. It was both wonderful and scary. With all these hopes pinned on me, there was no room for failure now.

Ang Tshering Sherpa, the chairman of the Asian Trekking agency had already arrived to meet me. He was a cheerful man who clicked my photos and wished me best of luck before leaving. After this we headed for the hotel, passing through Kathmandu markets on the way. For adventure seekers the Nepal capital is heaven. There are beer bars, restaurants and massage parlours for those who can pay. Almost every house in Kathmandu seems to have such bars or parlours. I saw various beautiful, colourful liquor bottles that were displayed outside prominent shops. Though I had never tasted liquor, I was informed by male members of my group that those bottles cost a fortune. We then headed for our hotel where after a brief rest we visited Kathmandu's narrow lanes to search for equipment one would require on the icy-rocky mountain. You have to have a really sharp eye to decipher the real from the fake in these Kathmandu markets – especially if you are looking for stuff that mountaineers need.

The shops here are full of original-looking fakes. On the Everest you can't afford to take a chance. Throughout the day we walked around, assessed the available stuff and compared their price and authenticity. Bachendri Pal, being an expert mountaineer, didn't want to rely on untested stuff. She ensured that we picked up the best equipment. There were many occasions where we thought we could do with cheaper, local stuff. On such occasions Pal was very firm. She told us that on the mountains it wasn't advisable to rely on untested stuff for even a minor mistake could prove fatal. We picked up jackets, undergarments, knives, headlights (forehead torches), special mountaineering shoes, crampons (equipment fitted on the shoe soles to help maintain a grip on the ice besides other stuff), ice axes, rope and several other things. We also packed some edible stuff. Not everything can be eaten on the mountains so we picked up roasted peanuts, Maggi and other such dry stuff that lasts long at that altitude.

In Kathmandu, you don't get chapattis easily. Vegetarian food too is hard to find and Baba Jagdeo Prasad who had accompanied us was a pure vegetarian.

After much difficulty we did locate a small hotel run by a Sikh where Baba had dal and chapattis. The price was exorbitant. But we had little choice. Baba realized this and for the remaining period of his stay here – he stayed for four days – had food only twice, surviving mainly on biscuits, namkeens and *chana-chabaina* (roasted spicy rice). One day Sahib, Baba, Raj Kishore and Rahul were taking a stroll on the streets of Kathmandu when an agent of the dime-a-dozen clubs appeared out of nowhere and insisted on Baba taking a massage. He claimed that the masseurs in his club were experts who would make Baba 'young'.

'We will get you a massage from soft hands.' Uninitiated to this life, Baba got curious and started insisting like a child that he wanted to try it out. 'I want to have a massage. They are promising it will help reduce my age!' In his village the only massage Baba knew was the one that his barber gave him after a haircut. He had taken several of them so far but hadn't become any younger. Naturally he was more than excited. Eventually Sahib told him he was being taken for a ride and that he would lose all his money. Baba beat a hasty retreat and saved himself. All of us laughed at his innocence!

In Kathmandu I met two ladies who I really liked. Chinmoi Mukherjee, Bachendri Pal's friend from Kolkata, had come to Kathmandu on her invitation. Mrs Mukherjee was a self-confessed mountain lover. 'Please take me along every time you go on an expedition to any mountain,' she would say to Bachendri Pal. She was a good motivator too. Mrs Mukherjee had brought with her some Ganga *jal* (holy water from the Ganges) so that she could perform a puja at the famed Pashupatinath temple. She had great faith in God and hence was able to perform a puja with priestly ease.

'Every time you are up against any problem, please remember the Almighty. From the mountain, he appears much closer!' I smiled. Mrs Mukherjee was indeed a warm-hearted lady. She had an infectious smile. One evening an elderly lady of nearly seventy, called Elizabeth Hawley, came to visit me with a couple of journalists. She is a mobile encyclopaedia on the Everest. She lives in Kathmandu and always makes it a point to meet and interview those who set out to scale the great mountain peak.

She told us that if I was successful in my mission, I would become the first woman amputee to conquer the mighty mountain. We had a nice chat over dinner, with her translating for the foreign journalists. Soon the time came for me to set off. A Sherpa was asked to accompany me till I reached the Everest base camp from where my full-time Sherpa Neema Kancha was supposed to take over. I had to say goodbye to all the people who had come to see me off.

There was Sahib, who hadn't managed to get a sponsorship and hence couldn't accompany me though I desperately wanted him to. There was Mrs Mukherjee with whom I had bonded so well. But she too had neither money nor sponsorship to fund her mountain trip. My brother Rahul and Raj Kishore had financial constraints too. Baba had money but was physically constrained by age and health concerns. All this meant that I was going to be all alone on the mountain. As I embarked on the tough fifty-two-day expedition I had their good wishes for company: My belief in the Almighty, Sahib's encouraging words, Baba's blessings, Mrs Mukherjee's sage advice, Rahul's brotherly hug, my mother's warm memories, and the strong bond I shared with my elder sister.

I bid goodbye to my family and walked into Kathmandu airport and spent two hours there with fellow climbers Susen Mahato and Hemant Gupta.

Mahato was an instructor at the Tata Steel Adventure Foundation while Gupta was an IIT Bombay alumni and a manager with Tata Steel. The flight was delayed and the three of us spent the time chatting about the route to Lukla and about how many flights had crashed on the way to the mountain. I kept checking the flight status on the display board. After the flight had been delayed by over two hours, the display board indicated a final change for the day – CANCELLED.

As it turned out, it wasn't only our flight that had been cancelled. All the remaining flights for the day had been cancelled too and I wanted to spend the bonus time with family. But by the time I called them, they had left by road for India. Since they had travelled some distance I decided not to call them back. Feeling a touch low and lonely, I headed for the hotel where I was pleasantly surprised to find Bachendri Pal. She was to return to Delhi by air the next morning. That enabled me to snatch a few more hours of her precious company before I set out for Lukla. She too appeared happy to see me and said that the delay had provided me some additional time to steel myself. She was referring to mental strength more than physical capability. The physical aspect is important but at this point, it all boils down to mental fitness. Bachendri Pal re-emphasized the virtue of patience, of not hurrying in the mountains. They were her final pearls of wisdom and I collected them all before hitting the bed.

After a rather nervous sleep, I was ready the next morning for the airport. Before I left, Bachendri Pal embraced me. 'Go and conquer the Everest,' she said.

THERE HAVE BEEN ENDLESS INSTANCES OF BUDDING mountaineers getting lost, hundreds of them getting killed or failing to cope with the mountain's icy challenge which comprises altitude sickness, avalanches, rockslides, blizzards, falls and fatigue. I was told how corpses were buried in the snow especially in the 'death zone', which is how the area above 26,000 ft is usually referred to. There have been several tragedies on the Everest. In May 1996 a mountain storm claimed eight lives – one of the biggest tragedies reported on the Everest for a very long time. In 2009–10 as many as twenty Australians were reported lost in the mountains. Nevertheless the fact that so far around 4000-odd people have 'peaked' successfully – since New Zealander Edmund Hillary and Nepalese Tensing Norgay Sherpa set the trend in 1953 – proves that the risks have failed to stem the flow of mountain lovers. They come here hoping to be on top of the world, quite literally. Forget the Everest, even at Kathmandu airport which is situated at 1350 m (4429 ft) above sea level, one gets that 'high'.

The flight to Lukla was a memorable one. Unlike the flight till Kathmandu, where I had been sandwiched in the middle, this time I had a window seat. The one-hour flight meandered its way through the mountains and offered a rare treat for the eyes as we flew above breathtaking landscapes. The scenery was gorgeous – nature appeared to have rolled out a green carpet on the ground below.

Lukla airport, renamed Hillary Tensing airport in 2008, is where our flight had landed. It is considered one of the most dangerous airports in the world. Passengers clap each time a flight lands safely. That's because this narrow airstrip is located at a height of 2843 m (9325 ft). I thanked the Almighty for a safe landing.

Bachendri Pal had warned me to get our woollen clothes ready before we touched down and she was right. It was freezing outside. We were welcomed by light snowflakes that were showered upon us from the heavens. We headed for the hotel carrying our equipment with us. The first lesson that the mountain teaches you is that, irrespective of one's financial status, everyone is equal. The sooner one sheds attitude, the better. No one can show attitude to the mountain. I had rested for an hour when the Asian Trekking agency people announced that it was time to begin my Everest march. A short prayer later I began my march.

We set out on foot for a place called Phakding, 2622 m above sea level. It is from here that the Everest climb technically begins. It took me nearly three hours to reach there. The mobile networks were still working, so I regularly spoke to my family, my trainers, Bachendri Pal and others.

A Sherpa joined me here and explained to me the importance of the place and prepared me mentally for the hardships that one encounters along the way. However, he was a stopgap arrangement for Neema Kancha who was to be my regular Sherpa right till the top. By the time I reached the guest house my legs were swollen, especially the left one. I asked for some warm water to wash my legs and tried to heal the swelling as best as I could.

The guest house resembled a set from one of

those blockbuster Yash Raj films. The location was picturesque. The scenery was beautiful, with green mingling in the backdrop of mountains and a river. The cold was biting but the scenic setting made me forget my pain and the weather outside.

Bachendri Pal had advised us to spend as much time outside as we could, to acclimatize to the cold. The beautiful guest house where we put up was built entirely of wood and named after the place where it was located. Even though it was freezing outside, a huge chimney in the middle kept the rooms warm. The area doesn't get any power supply. People rely on solar power here. Yet, the rooms are kept warm even at night with the help of an indigenously designed coal-filled chimney. We had fried rice here. Rice, as we discovered, was the staple food in the mountains.

After tea in the morning, we set out again for the mountains. At around 4 p.m., we arrived at Namche Bazaar, which is located 3340 m above sea level and is considered to be the highest market in the world.

Mountaineers looking for last-minute supplies find everything they want here. But it's much more expensive. I discovered that when I purchased a traditional woollen cap. The cap seller had originally asked for

Rs 1000 (NPR) but I managed to bring it down to Rs 450 (NPR). Roaming around the marketplace I could sense that my body had slowly started acclimatizing to the mountain. Most of the hotels and guest houses in this market were manned by women. I felt good seeing that. Call it my bias, but whenever I see women do well in life, take the lead in making informed decisions or break male barriers, the woman inside me always smiles.

A shop offered a live photo session. It was very costly. They had some sample photos which looked brilliant. I clicked some but I was forced to delete them after the shopkeeper objected. But I promised that I would get a photo done on my return. A little above Namche Bazaar is the Nepal Army's area. Here the army had put up its own exhibition. I saw a skull of a yeti – *him manav* (also called Ice Man). Hotels in this town had the same chimney system, as we had encountered earlier at Phakding, to keep the rooms warm.

Next morning we set out for a steeper climb. I could see Buddhist monasteries and prayed on the way. Khumjumg, 3790 m above sea level, was our next destination – full of steep climbs and dangerous slopes.

It was very difficult for me. Even those who had both their legs would rest on this climb, but I kept moving. Even though I walked at a decent pace, I found that it usually took me all day to reach our next halt. We used to have lunch and warm water at small restaurants. I had started drinking warm water from Lukla itself to ensure protection from cold and cough.

If you catch a cold in the mountains it is unlikely that you will be able to reach the summit. Coughing happens in staccato bursts, making it nearly impossible for anyone to climb. I had learnt these things from Bachendri Pal's brother Rajendra Singh Pal (Raju), an expert mountaineer himself. His experiences and advice stayed in my mind and I was determined to stay healthy.

I was familiarizing myself with interesting bits of informative nuggets on Everest. Here are some: A tea on the mountains used to cost Rs 200 (NPR), chicken rice (with barely any chicken) used to cost Rs 500 (NPR). I have preserved some of these bills. As we climbed up, even a litre of warm water (that I filled up my bottle with) used to cost Rs 200. But it's like amrit, the elixir of life.

I learnt a lot about the world of Sherpas too. There

is, for instance, a village near Namche Bazaar known as the 'village of Sherpas'. Before 1953 it was considered a sin to climb the mountains. But after Tensing Norgay's climb, these Sherpas found a fresh source of income by accompanying mountaineers and playing their friend, philosopher and guide.

Sherpas, as I gathered, are usually from east Nepal and found employment with any one of the twenty-seven Nepalese agencies (as until 2013), that operated on the Everest. Asian Trekking, the agency which Tata Steel had tied up with for me, was one of them. They were to look after me for the entire fifty-two days that I was supposed to last on the mountain.

While every agency aims at getting most climbers enrolled with them, the goodwill and ability of the Sherpas to cooperate with the climbers and ensure their safe return is what really determines the business that an agency generates. Along with one's will, talent and perseverance, one also needs a good Sherpa to survive in the mountains.

In 2013 around 297 people tried to climb the Everest. Barely 97–98 climbers succeeded. I was the lone amputee; since 2011 no amputee – male or female – has climbed. There were some people who had attempted it but had not been able to go beyond the base camp.

After Khumjumg we reached Tengboche (3837 m above sea level). I was already feeling tired. At Tengboche there is a big Buddhist monastery. Since I was following everything very closely I even remember the mantra that was chanted there. This is also the last place where one gets phone connectivity. Hillary and Tensing Norgay had taken the same route to the mountain and that is Tengboche's claim to fame.

Here I observed a rather interesting incident. I saw a yellow-billed chough, a crow-like bird, trying to sit on a telephone tower but the strong winds kept pushing it away. After some time, the bird decided to change its strategy. Instead of trying to land on the tower, it flew and sat a little ahead of it. The Everest and its surrounding peaks are home to a variety of animals and birds but only in the lower regions. The Sagarmatha National Park which is in the Everest region supports more than 150 species of birds, all found only in the lower ranges. Barring some jumping spiders, which are found even beyond 20,000 ft, and a couple of other snow-resistant varieties like bar-headed geese, no insect or animal or mammal life is visible after that height.

I too was finding things hard as I climbed higher. As oxygen levels decrease and eventually disappear, the mountain really tests even the best climbers. It took me a full day to travel from Tengboche to Dingboche (4343 m). Though there is no phone connectivity here, the Sherpas know of a point where one can stand and connect with the outside world. It's strange. If you move even a little the signal is lost but the moment you arrive at that point one can talk again.

Dingboche is also known as the village of Tensing Norgay. There are two routes from here, one that takes people to the Everest base camp and another that leads to Island Peak. To acclimatize to the climate and to the trek, I decided to do Island Peak before the Everest base camp.

Many people don't do this as everyone wants to cut travel time on the mountain. But Bachendri Pal had advised me not to take any shortcuts on the mountain. I was thus mentally prepared for the long haul.

FROM DINGBOCHE, OUR NEXT DESTINATION WAS Chhukung (4730 m above sea level). There we put up with a family whose house seemed to be the only one in the area. The house was managed by a woman even as her husband slept through the day. The main source of income for her family, as is for others like hers, is through mountaineers like me. The period between March and mid-June is when their business flourishes. The couple had a small naughty child with red cheeks. It appeared as if the child hadn't bathed in a long time. Looking at the icy surroundings it was clear that taking a bath wasn't easy. And the higher I climbed, the more expensive warm water became.

From Chhukung I was now travelling to Island Peak (located at 20,299 ft or 6189 m) to acclimatize myself. Ahead of Island Peak I spent a night at the Island base camp where I met several foreigners including some bigwigs like the chairman of the Audi group. I remember meeting several influential people but somehow, amid the icy, stony surroundings, important designations seem to melt. After all no one is taller than the mountain.

From the Island base camp I set out on the seemingly unending trek to Island Peak at night. All the climbers, with head masks, gears and headlights in place, moved upwards in one straight line. It was a majestic sight; people moving in a single line with torches strapped on the forehead giving the impression of a halo around the climbers. In nature's embrace, it appeared to me that the higher we climbed, the closer we came to that Almighty power.

Some people were behind me, while some ahead. After a while even those behind me started overtaking me. We reached Island Peak's crampon area after which we moved to the ice area.

Walking became extremely difficult from this point as the entire area was very slippery. One careless step and there were chances of sliding down to the rocky area with a force that would have broken all the bones in my body. I prayed on the move. They say God tests everyone here. I also travelled some distance by either sliding down or moving up a rope. The 'ropeway' is not easy, especially if you are climbing. Imagine several people hanging from a rope from the top of a mountain. A 9-mm rope can hold 2000 kg of weight.

I was having great difficulty making my way upwards as it was difficult to find a grip on the ice. After several hits my feet got a grip on the snow. Because I had a rod in my right leg, it wasn't easy for me to apply the kind of power that was required to displace the hard snow to gain a foothold. At times when I tried to hit the snow with my artificial left leg, it used to turn around at 180 degrees under the impact. Imagine hanging from a cliff in that position. Now until I adjusted that leg to its normal position, movement wasn't easy. I used to twist and turn my body at odd angles to be in a position to hold and fix my left leg by detaching the stump from my body and readjusting it – hanging in the air all the while.

I still shudder when I think of what could have happened had the stump slipped and fallen thousands of feet down into the valley. Had that happened, I would have been stuck up there in thin air, perhaps forever. There was another problem. It was very hard to hold on to the rope with my hands while hitting my feet against the snow and pulling my body upwards. Now I know the exact meaning of an 'uphill task'. There were moments when there was heavy bleeding from my legs.

Seeing the bleeding and the pain that I was in, my Sherpa got scared and suggested that I return. I laughed at the suggestion. I hadn't come this far to return. After about three hours of hit-and-miss, I climbed nearly 500 ft, equivalent to a five-storeyed building.

I was plagued with moments of doubt – and sometimes thought that I wouldn't be able to move any more. On the rope, whenever I got stuck, I tried the same desi techniques I used as child to prevail over Rahul when he used to push me down from a tree and I would hold on by entangling myself in the branches. Even as I kept moving, fighting my pain and fears, I noticed that many weighed down by the vagaries of nature also needed a push.

Ramlal, who was a member of our group, was one such person. He wasn't well and had been vomiting in the rather testing conditions. After some time he virtually signalled his inability to move any further. I saw him slump on the ice. This wasn't a good sign.

He needed some encouragement and out here this is something that is in short supply. So I slowed down as I approached him and told Ramlal not to give up and to accept the challenge.

Ramlal nodded weakly. Having made a mental leap, he soon overcame physical limitations too and started moving. Sometimes when you help someone else, you also end up helping yourself. I found myself more motivated even as I pushed Ramlal on. Even though we had moved some distance, the yellowish vomit was still clearly visible on the sparkling ice! On the mountain even a speck of dirt shows up.

By now icy winds had arrived. Blowing at a speed of over 200 km per hour, they tested our resolve but after some time they relented and slowed. The weather hadn't fully cleared as we approached Island Peak but it started clearing by the time we reached there. I wasn't aware that I had already created a record by being the first amputee ever to climb Island Peak. Experts say that scaling this peak is more difficult and technical than scaling the Everest. Having seen both, I can confirm this.

I was very happy to notice that even Ramlal had climbed alongside me. He had witnessed how I had kept moving despite the heavy bleeding from the wounds and the swelling in my legs. For Ramlal this was reason enough to feel inspired, something which he admitted to several times.

Having climbed the peak we immediately turned back towards the Island base camp. I now realized that I had been walking for nearly twelve hours without any food. This is not uncommon in the mountains as one is totally at nature's mercy here. Desperate to have something to silence the hunger pangs, I suddenly remembered that I had a boiled egg and some chocolates. I unpacked the bag to discover that the egg had frozen by now. The ice that had settled on the egg needed to be cleared first. I was busy doing that when I noticed a pair of hungry eyes looking at me. It was a yellow-billed chough, who had clearly not got anything to eat for a while. I shared some of my chocolates and the egg yolk with it.

I had begun the climb in darkness. Now encountering it in the light of day, I was really amazed that I had passed through such a dangerous route. A shiver ran down my spine at the thought of how close to death I had been the whole time. We finally arrived at the Island base camp at 6 p.m. It had turned very dark and I had my dinner here – my first full meal in several hours.

Answering the call of nature here was quite a challenge for me. That was because due to my handicap I couldn't sit on the Indian-style toilet seats and had to literally 'stand and deliver'. Another problem I faced was handling my menstruation. It was a challenge to do this in the mountains anyway and given my handicap, the task was not only painful but embarrassing too.

My right leg had swollen. There was no one around whom I could call for help. So I nursed my leg with a bottle of warm water. I don't know when I fell asleep remembering the Almighty and counting beads in his name. I kept my bottle inside a sleeping bag to make sure it remained warm. Had I left it outside, it would have frozen.

Eventually I learnt to carry the pain with me to bed and to sleep through it. In the morning I would wake up to the twitter of the Everest birds with whom I had developed a strange bond. Seeing them before getting up from bed had become part of my daily routine.

I again set out for Dingboche, passed through the same solitary house in Chhukung, met the same naughty child and even played with him. Before leaving, I also got a picture of the two of us together.

By 4 p.m. next day I reached Dingboche. The guest house here was covered in snow. In March, as the trekking season begins, these houses turn into guest houses. They have a dilapidated look from the outside. But from the inside it feels like a five-star hotel. Even in such icy-cold conditions, the temperature inside is warm and that makes the stay worth it.

Of course there is a price to the facility on offer but then there are times when one looks beyond money, especially on a mountain where not many options are available anyway. I could see various signed T-shirts and flags of different nations pasted on the walls of these guest houses. They were left by people on their return as a proof of their visit here.

I left a signed T-shirt gifted to me by Shahnaz Hussain there. At Chhukung there was a common toilet. Given my limitations, it was really difficult for me to adjust, especially since everyone appeared to be in a hurry to 'occupy the toilet'. But by now I had become accustomed to problems. At Fheriche (4270 m) I saw patches of greenery. This was the last bit of green on the way to the peak. From here on, as we set out for the Everest base camp via Lobuche, we barely saw any greenery.

I didn't stop for long at Lobuche and after some snacks I set out for the Everest base camp. Walking amidst the rock and snow, one got a feeling as if a great ice-army was trying to prevent human beings from moving any further. It was bitterly cold and the conditions here really tested one's spirit. On the way to the Everest base camp, one can see the Everest peak on a clear sky from a particular point. Fortunately the weather was clear when I arrived at that point. As my Sherpa pointed to the spot, I froze.

It was a thrilling view. I didn't know what awaited me – a successful visit to the top and a safe climb down, or an icy grave. All I wanted now was to reach the point that was visible to me from here. I said a silent prayer – '*Hum aayen aur aapka darshan kar paayen* (Bless us O mountain so that I am able to reach you).' We were glued to the sight until the Sherpa urged us to move. He said, 'Right now you have just got a view. But remember you have to reach there. So move!'

The narrow path we were now taking posed a big challenge, perhaps the biggest one so far. There was a cliff on one side and a rocky mountain wall on the other. From the rock side, small- to medium-sized stones rolled down at regular intervals. Falling from a height they had enough momentum to cause grievous injuries to anyone they fell on. One couldn't move away as the other side was open. It was like choosing between injury and death. It is here that one feels dwarfed by nature.

I really believe that it was divine intervention that kept me safe during such occasions. If I am here today, it's proof that some power was protecting me and helping me move. The base camp fortunately appeared soon after this rather nerve-wracking phase. So far there had been barely a couple of climbers who had walked either alongside or ahead of me. But now I couldn't believe my eyes as the base camp appeared on the horizon.

A carnival-like atmosphere prevailed there. Sherpas had put up mantra-flags here as proof of their group's arrival. Such flags are put up at all the major spots on the mountain to mark a successful trip. A Sherpa is the happiest person on the mountain when his group successfully reaches the destination. That's because their price and their credibility to manage their climber (group) also goes up after every successful climb.

Their price also depends on the kind of climber they accompany. For instance, my Sherpa Neema Kancha who accompanied me to the top and back – it is from this base camp that he accompanied me – should now be among the 'top ten' Sherpas of Everest.

One of the flags said, 'Eco Everest 2013'. An Eco Everest expedition, of which I too was a part, is one in which climbers are supposed to ensure that they don't contribute to dirtying the mountain. Here, after answering the call of nature, one was required to pack the waste in a pouch and bury it in the snow after writing one's name on the waste-pouch. On our return we would be required to dig them out, identify our packet and take it downhill. I was really happy that I was part of the Eco expedition, for the Everest is now full of tons of waste, largely comprising empty oxygen bottles, human waste, damaged or unused climbing equipment. Now, the Nepal government has woken up to the problem and is doing its bit to clean up the mountains. I learn that now even a waste incinerator has been installed up there. All these are much-needed steps and I would love to associate myself with the task of making people aware of the need to keep the mountains clean.

It was a strange coincidence. As I arrived at the Everest base camp, I remembered the date – 11 April 2013. Exactly two years had passed since I had been thrown out of a moving train. Remember, none can defeat you until you concede. Yes, occasional failures will test you but keep trying. Some door of opportunity will certainly open.

AT THE BASE CAMP, I HAD TO GO STRAIGHT TO ASIAN Trekking's dining camp. I didn't trip anywhere, even though it was one of the more difficult routes. But on my way to the dining tent I slipped and hurt myself. It was nothing more than a bruise but it made me realize that one should never take anything for granted in the mountains.

At the camp, I met the oldies of Asian Trekking and several foreigners. Most of them didn't know that I was handicapped. I also didn't think it was important to tell them about it. It was purely by chance that this fact came to light.

I was trying to spend as much time outside the camp as possible in order to make sure my body adjusted to the high altitude. I regularly arrived late in the evening. One day, while returning, my artificial leg got wet with snow because I had slipped a couple of times on the slippery surface.

Next morning I left the artificial leg out in the sun to dry. I think this was when some foreigners realized that I had only one leg. After that my TRP soared. I was inundated with requests from them to talk to their relatives on Skype. I did.

But as I spoke to their families, I longed to connect with my family too. I thought of requesting some of them to arrange for a Skype call with my family. But then I realized that to make the call, my family too should be on Skype. While I could have made a satellite call home, all this was too expensive and cumbersome. In any case, I knew that my family would be really happy to see me on top of the Everest.

At the base camp there was a foreign couple who had intended to climb only till this point. They were also from Asian Trekking so they were staying in the same camp as me. When they heard about me, they came over to visit. However, I was away when they dropped by and left a letter, some chocolates, their contact number and their blessings for me. The letter made me emotional. It was written so well that I couldn't control my tears.

All alone on the mountains, fighting pain and tears on a daily basis had made me a touch cynical. The letter came as a welcome relief, soothing my frayed nerves and tattered emotional state. At least someone had truly connected with me. I stayed for a month at the base camp with two Haryana Police girls for company. They too desired to conquer the Everest. They used to take bath every day – something I wanted to do as well. But I had heard stories of how people catch a cold on the mountains. Once you catch a cold here, it doesn't go away easily, making climbing next to impossible. I preferred to sponge my body with warm water instead.

Kancha, my mountain guide, was a nice and helpful Nepalese man who, at times, even used to scold me if he got upset. His main role began after Camp 4. You won't believe how the kitchen staff used to get water for us there! Whenever water was needed, they would walk on the ice up to a particular spot where they would start scratching the icy surface. Slowly, the ice would give way and there would be water underneath.

For a climber, identifying such spots is crucial for survival. If you put pressure on such surfaces, chances are that you will get sucked into the icy-cold water and, once there, it won't be easy to get out. That's why the role of Sherpas is so important on these mountains.

At the base camp I used to declare that I would cook Maggi the way it's done in the Hindi heartland. I used to spice it up nicely besides adding vegetables. Many of them liked whatever I cooked. The kitchen staffers, they too took good care of me. Every time they cooked a special dish like chicken they used to save some for me even if I was away.

Living with foreigners had helped me pick up some English. I had started making an effort to learn the language. As I interacted with them, I also witnessed some of them romancing on the mountains. A foreign couple who had become friends during their mountain trip had become a hot topic of discussion. They seemed to be madly in love. But their love didn't last long. Soon we started witnessing quarrels and heated exchanges of words. The girl accused the boy of having cheated her. They stopped talking to each other. Things became so ugly that the Asian Trekking agency staff had to intervene. The boy had sponsored the girl. But now she suspected him of having an ulterior motive in doing that.

Finally, the boss of the Asian Trekking agency intervened after the two didn't mend their ways despite a warning. 'Your journey ends here,' he declared. The youth shrugged and agreed. He asked for a helicopter and got one for a price. The girl didn't have any money. So she had to go down crying and on foot with only a Sherpa for company. I was told that such friendships and break-ups were quite common on the Everest.

Sandwiched between the base camp and Camp 1 is the majestic and dangerous Khumbu glacier known for its spectacular icefall. It is the highest glacier in the world, and is witness to several triumphs and tragedies. The gaps on the glaciers kept fluctuating which meant one could not afford to make an error. One has to time one's jump to perfection, for if you get stuck in the crevices it simply means a badly battered and bruised body *if* one survives. Neema Kancha, my Sherpa, used to cross the crevices using a rope and an ice axe. After crossing, he would call me to the other side. For a normal person it would be easy to jump. But what was normal for others was very difficult for me. Still, in a month's time I had climbed most of the small and medium peaks around Camp 1 (Khumbu glacier) area. Now I was ready for the real thing.

WE HAD BARELY CROSSED HALF THE DISTANCE between Camp 1 and Camp 2 when we sighted our immediate destination. Camp 2 appeared to be just ahead but, in reality, it was farther away. In the mountains you rarely move straight for long. The curvaceous hilly routes make you walk farther than it seems. To ensure that boredom and frustration don't set in during such times, it's important to engage your mind. Bachendri Pal's advice came in handy here. She had advised me to count the number of steps I could take in one go. I remember taking 500 steps in one go. Such small yet effective tips kept me going, ensuring that on many occasions I was ahead of the able-bodied climbers too. I remember passing on the 'count steps' tip to fellow climbers like Ramlal and Kanta.

Staying mentally healthy is one of the keys to success

here – where nature tests your resolve, your ability to stay focused at every step. It isn't easy. That's why we have so many unsuccessful attempts. But I think one should rid one's mind of all negative energies. Just play along, secure in the belief that even fate favours the truly committed and the brave.

At around 1 p.m. we reached Camp 2 where we rested awhile. The long trek from Camp 1 to Camp 2 on the snow had resulted in my boots getting wet. So I removed the crampon and changed the lower as it too was soggy.

After this we headed towards the dining hall where bread, butter, jam along with packaged soup, eggs and beef were available. Mountain-fruit juices were also available. We also got some rice which we ate with oil and salt. But for me, more precious than anything else was warm water which I drank the most throughout my stay on the mountains. Out here I stayed with Anita, the Haryana Police girl. Though I was mostly alone, the small group of fellow climbers like Anita, Ramlal and Kanta – also from Haryana Police – had bonded well.

Camp 3 was our next destination. We got excited like children as soon as someone announced that Camp 3 was visible with the help of binoculars. Greedy-eyed, we took turns to watch our next stopover. I could understand this excitement. Everyone was now travelling mentally, taking giant leaps to the Everest top. Throughout our two-day stay at Camp 2 our eyes remained glued to Camp 3, where we were headed to next. I remember going to sleep while gazing at Camp 3. And after waking up I would again focus on the camp that was located at a very high altitude. Finally, at around 1.30 at night, we set out for Camp 3 planning to reach there by 12.30 the next afternoon.

So far I had not put on the oxygen mask though I could see other climbers having problems in breathing. However, Kancha insisted that I use the mask to prevent energy loss. I wasn't interested as I was not having any breathing problems till now. But since my Sherpa persisted, I finally put the oxygen mask on. The moment I put it on, I started experiencing problems. Finally I had to take it off and as soon as I did so, I felt better. I covered the entire stretch between Camp 2 and Camp 3 without the help of an oxygen mask but as soon as I reached my destination I experienced a dip in oxygen levels.

Neema Kancha now suggested that I put the mask on and this time I readily obeyed his advice. To camp here, the ice had to be cleared first. As advised by Kancha, I went to sleep with the oxygen mask on. The Sherpa had told me that if I didn't put it on throughout the night, I would become extremely weak.

Sherpas, however, don't require these masks at least till Camp 3; they use them from Camp 4 onwards. Having been born and brought up in the mountains, they are comfortable in conditions that others find taxing. We used to anchor ourselves with ropes and walk with crampon-studded boots even for answering the call of nature. The terrain is highly dangerous and very slippery. We were told that not many climbers prefer to stay long at this camp because the fear of an avalanche or ice walls sliding down is quite high at this point.

From this height the mountain roads down below looked like thin lines and climbers looked like ants. As time passed, our excitement rose. We desperately wanted to move on to Camp 4 but the problem was that as the heights increase and climbers slow down, people take time to vacate their camps. Our Sherpas were regularly in touch with their counterparts at Camp 4 and were informing us that the camp had still not been vacated. After several hours our

Camp 3 Sherpas finally announced that it was time to move. We set out at 1 a.m. to reach Camp 4 at 1 p.m. after walking continuously for twelve hours. Our timing was excellent. Reaching Camp 4 by 1 p.m. is considered good, simply because one is required to set out for the Everest on the same night.

The moment we arrived at Camp 4, we were greeted with the rather depressing and sad news of a Korean girl's death. We never learnt the details of the incident. We also heard that another mountaineer, whose lungs had filled up with water, had died in the adjacent tent. All this was enough to terrify anyone.

Even sleeping in the mountains in these heights is not considered safe. That's why I didn't sleep despite having time on my hands. I was ahead of Ramlal and Kanta till Camp 4 though Anita had left earlier with Mahato. I set out for the summit at 4 p.m. on 20 May 2013 along with Ramlal and Kanta. Everybody was in bad shape but my condition had really started deteriorating now.

I had been leading Ramlal and Kanta by a fair margin till Camp 4, but I trailed them now. They overtook me on the way to the summit during which we encountered blue ice – the very slippery ice that tires even the best climbers out. I had little energy left in me to keep a grip on it. This effort drained me of a lot of energy. Both my legs were swollen and in bad shape, especially because I had covered the entire stretch from Camp 3 to Camp 4 by continuously hitting my crampon against the snow. Now it seemed that my legs, especially the left one, had hardly any strength left.

TO MAKE MATTERS WORSE MY HANDS HAD SEVERAL cuts and even my artificial left leg stump had been damaged. Banging my feet against the snow to get a grip on the ice simply reopened old wounds. I was bleeding once again. Running out of ideas and options, I asked my Sherpa to hold my hand. To my surprise he refused. Naturally I was angry, shocked and very hurt. How could my guide be so insensitive? What I didn't realize then was that the Sherpa probably wanted to tell me to be brave and manage things on my own at this point, when we were still some distance away from the summit.

I was so angry and hurt at the guide's refusal that I let go of the rope I was holding and declared that I wouldn't move an inch. I felt like crying. The pain had intensified by now. The bleeding made the situation worse.

Yet, despite my words, I found myself moving forward. It was as if I was being pushed by an invisible force. After this I decided that, come what may, having come so close, I wouldn't leave without a fight. My emotional outburst had delayed me and most of the other members of my group had overtaken me by now.

I took nearly ninety minutes to cross the blue ice. My fellow climbers had disappeared deep into the snow. Inside my leather jacket I could feel the small bead garland that I used to count the number of times I remembered God. Providing the additional spiritual push were the trident, the photos of Swami Vivekananda, Ramakrishna Paramhansa and Maa Sharda Devi that were still with me. I kept telling myself, 'The Lord is with me . . .'

After some time I realized that the blue ice had given way to soft ice which made walking a bit easier. I walked on the soft ice for some time before arriving at a stretch that was part snow, part rock. Now, this was an extremely difficult point to manoeuvre as every time I hit the crampon to get a grip, my feet used to invariably hit the rocky surface making me double up in pain.

On several occasions my artificial leg actually turned 180 degrees. I was constantly getting delayed since I had to regularly stop to adjust it back to its normal position. More people had begun to overtake me by now. It was around 1 a.m. when I recognized that one of the climbers approaching me from behind was an Indian.

His name was Loveraj Dharam Sattu and he had climbed the Everest three times. I had briefly interacted with him during my stay at Camp 4. He was also the leader of the group but, strangely enough, I was seeing him for the first time since Camp 2. As he crossed me, he remarked, 'Arrey, you are still here!'

I nodded and requested him to climb with me. But Sattu was in a hurry to post his presence at the top for the fourth time. So he moved on. This happened near the 'balcony area' – where I was now reaching after walking continuously for almost sixteen hours since leaving Camp 4.

My Sherpa was required to cut down his speed to match mine. I wanted to move at a decent pace as faster movement also helps in blood circulation. I had now arrived at the Hillary step, one of the most difficult stretches of the Everest.

The biggest problem that one encounters in this stretch is that one has to cross a temporary rocky surface wearing a crampon. Negotiating the rocky area wearing a crampon is difficult. Crampons are required to aid you in walking on ice. But on rocky surface they become a liability.

Despite this obvious disadvantage, climbers don't take them off. That's because, shortly after the rocky surface, one again encounters snow where the crampon is a must. Thus, despite crampons hindering my movement and making it risky too (they used to slide on the rocks), I continued to walk.

This effort aggravated the bleeding in my legs. I was in really bad shape and was still trying to increase my speed when I heard some climbers celebrate. They were none other than Ramlal, Kanta and others who were now on their way back. I was so exhausted that even recognizing fellow climbers was becoming difficult. I was moving like a drunkard. There was ice all around me and over me, on and inside my jacket, my boots, my face mask, and oxygen cylinder. I was losing energy fast. Ramlal and Kanta, now returning with the rest of the group, thought I wouldn't survive. They wanted me to come down. 'The record is still going to be yours. No female amputee has come even this far,' they said.

I spotted Sattu again, who was now returning after completing the summit. Seeing my condition he said, 'Arunima, return now.' Perhaps he was scared that I wouldn't last. I remember telling him, 'Sir, please wait for me. We could climb down together.' Ignoring my request, Sattu moved down leaving me in a state of shock. My initial reaction was that of disbelief. How could a group leader ignore the request made by his group member?

With hindsight I now realize that it was practically impossible for anyone to hold on for that long. I would have taken at least three hours to do the summit and return. At that altitude it is next to impossible for anyone to hold on, that too for as long as I had expected him to. Meanwhile my Sherpa asked me if I could move. I nodded.

From the point where I stood, I could see a huge queue of climbers waiting for their turn to move on. For those who are used to traffic jams in the country's major cities, this was a unique sight – a human traffic jam on the mountain. Apparently the route to the

Everest was dangerously narrow. On one side there was rock and on the other, a deadly cliff. One had to walk down an extremely slippery and narrow path. This was time-consuming since only one person could cross at a time. Oxygen was running out fast. My Sherpa helped me regulate the flow to ensure that it lasted longer. In about two hours the jam cleared. A little ahead, an even steeper and narrower climb awaited me.

I slipped and fell once. The anxiousness was beginning to show. My Sherpa said I must quit. But I knew that there was no going back from this point. We were between the south summit and the Hillary step when my Sherpa first warned me about the depleting oxygen levels and suggested – yet again – that I quit. The Sherpa wasn't to blame. I could sense that my condition was deteriorating badly. Having failed to persuade me, Neema Kancha decided to inform my agency leader. 'If she doesn't quit now, she will die,' I heard him say on his wireless talkie.

He spoke for a while, his voice betraying his concern. Word about my refusal to quit hadn't just spread on the mountain but my family in UP and Bachendri Pal in Jharkhand too had learnt the news. Even as the emotional drama played out near the Everest top, my legs had started turning cold. This wasn't a good sign. Frustrated at my refusal to follow his warning, my Sherpa shouted at me, 'I too want to live!' My agency leader spoke to me on a satellite phone, 'Arunima, you have already posted a world record; please come back.' This was something rare – a female amputee pushing on, against everyone's advice.

I was thinking beyond records now. Bachendri Pal's words were ringing in my ears, 'Arunima, every time you feel that you won't be able to move forward any more, just look back and think how far you have come and how little you have to go forward to achieve your goal!' My nose had started bleeding. I still had complete faith in my equipment, people's blessings and most importantly, in God.

There were so many for whom I had become a ray of hope, an inspiration. Now I had to climb the top not just for my sake but to ensure that the belief that others had in my ability wasn't shattered. Again Pal's words rang in my ears – 'When you met me for the first time it was just your dream. Now it's no longer just your dream. It's Tata Steel's dream. It is the country's dream.' I also remembered Rahul and Sahib and the way both had gone out of their way to ensure that I climbed.

Since that fateful night when I was pushed from a moving train by some greedy wolves, nothing had been easy for me or my family. In fact even before the train tragedy, my life had been one of struggle. We have had to always fight our way for everything. My climb till this point too hadn't been easy. I had given everything for this moment so that I could live my dream – a dream that was as much mine as it was that of my family. It was a moment the world was waiting to hear about. I remembered the Delhi press conference and the doubts that were expressed about my ability. Few have come this far. So far only 4000-odd people have managed to scale the peak since 1953. If I succeeded I would be the first in my category ever to do so. A world record awaited me.

I PUSHED FORWARD EVEN AS MY SHERPA KEPT INSISTING that I return. I remember telling him that if he wanted to return he could do so but there was no way I was going back now. 'I have enough oxygen to reach the summit and hoist the country's flag. What happens after that doesn't matter any more,' I told my beleaguered Sherpa. Actually reaching the top was not the only issue at hand. Many climbers, having scaled the Everest, have succumbed on their way down simply due to lack of oxygen, exhaustion, overexcitement or sheer carelessness.

I don't know if my words had any effect on him but I could see Neema Kancha following me even as I continued to drag myself to the top. I kept on dragging myself for what I thought was a very long time. The 'drag walk drag' continued till it finally happened. Atop a small 20x20 ice table, I saw several flags of various countries fluttering proudly. I had lived this moment so many times in my mind that I didn't have to be told that finally, I had arrived.

At 10.55 a.m. on 21 May 2013, I was on top of the world.

I felt like dancing, crying and laughing at the same time. My mind was a kaleidoscope of emotions. I knelt down, utterly exhausted. I felt like shouting, announcing my arrival to the world. Everyone has a reason to be alive, a role to fulfil. Maybe this was mine. Out here on the ice-table top I looked around for a pole to hoist my country's flag. Since there weren't any, I held my flag and raised both my hands high up to symbolically register my country's record. My Sherpa and I then prayed before a Tibetan flag of the Lamas on which some mantras were written. I kissed my gods who had accompanied me and left them there after offering prayers before them. They had given me a lot of strength and hope.

I was taking time. Most others who had climbed with me had left. I was alone with my Sherpa now. Suddenly I started feeling a little uneasy. My head started spinning and I felt very weak. Barely able to stand, I rested myself against the small ice top. Just then I noticed another Sherpa. I don't really know how he came there. One doesn't usually find a spare Sherpa atop the Everest. But I was used to miracles by now. The mysterious Sherpa gave me an energy gel that was wrapped in a pouch. Despite the obvious joy, I was very weak with hardly any strength left in me to even tear the gel wrapper. He helped me tear the pouch and consume the gel even as I rested against a mountaintop. The gel made me feel a little better almost immediately.

While I recovered, the new Sherpa prepared to leave. As if reading my mind which was curious to know how he was here, he said he had come to the top with an English climber who left early. That's why, he said, he had some spare energy gel left. As a child I had heard stories of how God used to help his devotees in mysterious ways. For me this Sherpa was a godsend. Imagine getting an energy boost at the highest point in the world. While the gel helped me stand, the Sherpa quickly descended. I had now started walking with the help of an ice wall and my head wasn't spinning any more.

Somehow I was sure that I wouldn't die; not

anymore. On the Everest, trying to reach the top after 11 a.m. is not considered wise. They call it the 'suicide attempt' here as the weather really turns bad soon after. My Sherpa frantically gestured to me to hurry before the oxygen ran out. But instead of following him, I did something that made my guide visibly faint.

'Wait, I have something else to do now,' I told Neema. As he looked quizzically at me, I patiently told him that I would like him to make a video of me in my phone. Neema appeared bewildered. He had seen climbers run for their lives, hurrying down after reaching the top, but none willing to risk their life for a video. He had no option but to do what I had asked him to. In the short ninety-second video, I simply said, 'I am very happy today. I firmly believe that if you have set your mind to achieve something, you should pursue it. Nothing is impossible for a truly determined person . . .'

I had a reason for recording the video. Though I had felt a divine force rescue me on several occasions, out here on this icy top, I didn't want to take any chances. There were far too many people who wanted to hear from me on how it felt after reaching the top. It is for them that I got the video recorded; so that even if I was unable to reach them, this video would.

That wasn't all. Having made the video, Neema gestured to me to rush down. Everyone had left by this time. I was alone with the guide. 'Just one more thing now – I want to carry a stone from the Everest peak,' I told Neema, who now thought that he was destined to die with me.

I remember it was Bachendri Pal who had suggested that, in case I remembered, I should bring back a piece of the peak with me. The locals reverently refer to the top as *sagar matha* – which roughly translates to the 'head of the sea'. An agitated Neema struck his ice axe at the Everest with such great force that with one single blow he displaced more than 250 gm of the mountaintop. 'Now carry it,' he growled. The mountain piece was heavier than I had imagined. I asked him to break it in two but a livid Neema Kancha flatly refused.

I was aware that my oxygen cylinder had almost run out and that I had put my life as well as that of the Sherpa at stake. But I also had a strange feeling that if God had let me breathe so far, he would do something to rescue me again. And so it happened. A climber who had almost made it to the top thought it wise to return rather than make a 'post-11 a.m.-suicide attempt'. He was carrying two oxygen cylinders, one that he was using and another fresh one.

He took out the one he was using and replaced it with the fresh one. Before heading down he left his used cylinder there. Neema Kancha saw this and quickly fetched it for me. This spare oxygen was nothing short of a miracle. With renewed energy levels I now began the climb down. During the climb down one should be more careful than while climbing up. That's because joy, fatigue and carelessness often make for a killer combination on the way down.

This was evident from the corpses of those valiant climbers who had tried to climb till their last breath. For all you know, their luck might have run out on their way down. Some had 'red ice' on their faces. They had started bleeding before they died. As ice firmed up on their faces, it too attained a reddish hue. In fact I could even spot some people who were alive and half buried in the snow. The scenes were scary. There was one person who was alive but had now given up all hope. I remember shaking one such person but he wouldn't budge an inch.

My Sherpa again warned me to ignore such things.

It was difficult but the Sherpa was right. I decided to slide down after tying myself with a rope. As I slid down facing the cliff side, my artificial leg became loose. As my nervous Sherpa shouted, I froze. I had survived death before but this was really scary as the route was highly dangerous. The silicone gel inside the artificial leg had become wet and that's why the leg had come loose. I somehow adjusted my stump and continued to move down though my artificial leg came off nearly twice or thrice. Under the icy-cold conditions the skin on my face too had started to peel off.

Suddenly there was heavy bleeding from my stump. My Sherpa was constantly urging me to move. I started crying. I had done the summit but now felt that I would not return alive. The corpses kept appearing before my eyes. Even my tears started freezing. I then uttered a prayer – 'I am your child. I won't give up.' Suddenly I felt a little better as I caught the rope and started dragging myself down. After a little while, when we reached a rocky area, I adjusted myself, took off my trousers, inners and readjusted the silicone gel inside the stump. Now, perhaps impressed by my commitment, Neema Kancha said, 'Arunima, I am with you. Don't worry, even if it means death, we will embrace it together. I won't run away.'

IT WAS 9 P.M. WHEN I SPOTTED MY TENT AT CAMP 4. At Camp 4 everybody was jubilant. But I was so tired that I shouted at the others to open the tent. My Sherpa opened my crampon. Each one of us was very tired. Both of us returned to our tent. It took nearly thirty minutes to take off my shoes. I was just unable to do it. The feeling of 'I have done it' was yet to sink in. My fingers had started turning black due to excessive cold. I needed warm water. My Sherpa advised me not to rush into warm water and to let my fingers adjust. I slowly changed.

Kanta, who was in my tent, was suffering from 'snow blindness'. She was crying bitterly. I too was feeling as much pain. I was in bad shape but I knew that I couldn't ignore Kanta's cries. As she cried like a child, I snubbed her. 'Hold on! You aren't the only one who is in pain. Everybody is.' I suggested some local remedy to her and it helped.

I now called out for some warm water. Icy winds had burned my face. So now all I did was to apply cream on my face as and when I could. My lips too used to get stuck during the climb and would take some time to warm up. I had some chocolates and slowly started to feel better.

Next day, as we moved down I realized that I still hadn't fully regained my energy – I had barely moved a foot when I fell. My Sherpa helped me stand up again. With his help, and a brand-new oxygen cylinder, I reached Camp 3 at nearly 3 p.m. I had set out from Camp 4 at 8 a.m. Here my tent was nowhere to be seen. That was because I was the last to arrive here. And it meant we had to head for Camp 2 now.

On the way when one of the Sherpas offered me a cold drink, I gulped down three to four glasses in one go. I had lived mostly on warm water. So when I had the locally prepared cold drink I liked its taste so much that I had several glasses of it. I thanked the Sherpa but within an hour or so I had started coughing. I realized my mistake of deviating from my strict schedule.

The coughing bouts grew in intensity as time wore on; so much so that having coughed all through the night, I had started vomiting blood by morning. Locals told me not to worry as this was a temporary phase and thankfully they were right.

Camp 2 had a regular kitchen. Everyone congratulated me on my conquest and I finally began to relax. After this I decided to go down to the base camp as soon as possible. I skipped Camp 1 and sometime between 4 p.m. and 5 p.m., I reached the base camp. The scene was very different from when I had left it. The ice had started melting. Tents had been taken off. Mine was the only tent that was still standing.

Ramlal, Kanta and Anita had left by helicopter. They were all from Haryana and had their own reasons to rush back. Ramlal wanted me to take a helicopter too. I couldn't afford air travel and moreover, I thought it wasn't right for a mountaineer to fly back. I distributed Rs 11,000 left with me at the base camp. Then I descended after having one last look at the mountain and my tent. On my way down some journalists from the foreign press found me. They had been looking for me to talk about my climb. I gave my first interview on my return in the mountains itself. Things became crazy from then on.

AROUND 11 A.M. I LANDED AT KATHMANDU AIRPORT from Lukla where Sahib met me. I was overjoyed to see him. From there we drove to the Indian embassy in Nepal where Jayant Yadav, the then ambassador to Nepal, welcomed me. From there we went to the Vaishali Hotel, where I met P.P. Kapadia, a manager at the Tata Steel Adventure Foundation who had come from Jamshedpur to receive me. From there we set out for Lucknow after making brief stopovers at Delhi and Ranchi where I addressed big press conferences organized by Tata Steel. In the meantime a Hollywood producer had called my family to ask for film rights.

At Lucknow airport nearly 2500 people had turned up to greet me. My jubilant family was there as well. They waved to me and shouted with joy the moment they saw me. I could see tears in their eyes.

But everyone was laughing too. This wasn't just a big day for me but one for them too. In fact my family later told me that the district magistrate and the senior superintendent of police of my native district Ambedkarnagar had visited my family to congratulate them on my world record. After spending a day in Lucknow we set out for Ambedkarnagar where a grand welcome awaited us.

Something kept bothering me throughout. It was my mother's absence at the airport. I wondered why my mother wasn't here to share my triumph. The thought remained till I finally met her in Ambedkarnagar. She met me at the doorstep with a smile and an advice that would stay with me forever. The advice was simple yet immensely powerful. 'Arunima, this is your high moment. I know you are on a high. But no matter how high your achievements, your feet should always be on the ground.' Her words had a magical effect. Whatever little ego I had developed due to my achievement and the subsequent accolades that started coming my way disappeared in no time. Even before I had set out on my Everest mission, when in fact I was looking for a sponsor, my mother had encouraged me to go for it, saying that if I failed to find a sponsor she would not hesitate to sell her Ambedkarnagar house to fund my dream if I was determined to pursue it.

Locals informed me that they hadn't witnessed such excitement in a very long time. My first destination was the Shiv Baba temple and I saw a huge crowd waiting for me there as well. People had even arranged for an open Gypsy so that I could greet people who had lined up on both sides of the road to greet me.

Local politicians, the district officials and some religious leaders had already arrived at home. The same day the then district magistrate announced that a lane would be named after me. For the next week or so, I felt on top of the world. Everyone wanted to see me. Many others came to consult me about how to excel in life. Each one of them thought that I had an answer to their questions! The best thing of all was to be at home and be spoilt. My family prepared the choicest of dishes for me. All these months I had resisted the temptation to eat too much. Now, I threw caution to the winds and ate like mad.

After a few days, I got a call from the UP chief minister Akhilesh Yadav. We went to Lucknow to meet him. A special welcome ceremony was organized at the CM's residence where Akhileshji felicitated me. He gave me a cheque of Rs 25 lakh for my achievement and another of Rs 1 lakh, which he said was for my 'personal expenses'. He said, 'You deserve it. We are proud of you.' After this I started receiving invites from one and all, people wanting to hear me.

In the meantime more greetings poured in – from the then PM Manmohan Singh, Lok Sabha Speaker Meira Kumar, Congress President Sonia Gandhi, the then sports minister Jitendra Singh (as Ajay Maken had taken a party post by then). I was later informed that PM Narendra Modi, who was the Gujarat chief minister then, was among the first politicians to acknowledge my feat through a tweet. Gradually, I realized that people had started seeing me as a motivational speaker. There were hundreds of invites seeking my participation and a talk on 'how I did it'.

I must admit that while I was enjoying this attention thoroughly, a part of me couldn't quite believe it. A little over a year ago, I was bleeding heavily on a railway track with no one to help me. Before that I had been hurrying to Delhi to try and secure a job for my desperate family. Everything had changed – most of all, my dreams and ambitions. I felt as if I had been born again – born again on the mountain.

EPILOGUE

WHILE I WAS INJURED AND CONVALESCING, I WITNESSED the love and support of many people. That's when it struck me that I too should do something to ensure that handicapped youths don't end up spending a life full of neglect and insecurity. Just because a part of them had been incapacitated didn't mean that they had nothing to look forward to. The idea of an International Sports Academy for the Handicapped was born out of this desire.

But we also knew that the academy was going to require a lot of time, a lot of effort and lots and lots of money. It is a very costly dream – worth more than Rs 25 crore. My god! That's a staggering amount for a lower-middle-class family like ours. Frankly speaking, we wouldn't even know how many zeros were required to write that figure.

When the idea was conceived, I was actually lying in my hospital bed worrying about how and who would fund my treatment. Sahib stepped in here. He said, 'Just as the Kashi Hindu University was set up by Madan Mohan Malaviya through donations, we too should ask for funds.' And just like at so many points in my life so far, this problem too was solved by divine intervention.

Within a couple of days, Uma Shankar Dixit, a resident of Bether, Unnao, arrived to make the first donation, of Rs 21,000. We took it as another sign that we should go ahead with our plan. How else do you explain a complete stranger walking in and offering to help? What's more, Dixitji also offered to supply all the bricks free of cost if we planned to establish our sports academy near Unnao! Eventually we did settle for Unnao and Dixitji has kept his promise.

Work on the academy project is now underway. I plan to look for young people who, instead of being weighed down by their troubles, are committed to making a mark in the world. I want to provide them with a complete package under one roof – from taking care of their stay to monitoring their training and education. The trainees will be selected from our villages. We will camp in villages, spending time to spot talent. We will train them in all indoor games and barring three, all outdoor games recognized in the Olympics.

The academy's board has been set up and named after the great freedom fighter Pandit Chandrashekhar Azad who hailed from Unnao. None of my blood relations are part of the board. It comprises people from seven different states, all of whom I met after I lost my leg on that fateful night. We have tried to stay clear of dynastic linkages and caste and language barriers. Arunima Foundation that will ultimately manage the Sports Academy too will soon be established.

NOW, EVERYWHERE I GO, I ALWAYS MAKE AN APPEAL to people to fund our dream. I've been lucky to meet some important people who have all committed to help.

Narendra Modiji hadn't become the prime minister of India when I first met him. He was the chief minister of Gujarat when he invited me to Gandhinagar after my record-breaking feat. I accepted the invite and visited Gujarat where I was felicitated by the charismatic leader. 'What's your next mission, Arunima?' he asked me. I was ready with the answer: 'Sports academy, sir. I need your support!' 'Sure, full support,' Modiji said. One of his ministers added, 'The moment our government is formed at the Centre, we will be in a position to sponsor several sports academies.' Now that the Modi government at the Centre is a reality, I really hope that the prime minister remembers his promise.

I also met Ratan Tata recently. The man needs no introduction, does he? The meeting took nearly a year to materialize but those forty minutes that I spent in his company were worth the wait. I felt shy as I went to the meeting and told him, 'I have been so anxious to meet you. But I was also really nervous.' To this the great man said, 'So was I!'

Many corporates like Microsoft, Tech Mahindra, Eldeco have also assured us of their support. The secretary of Ramakrishna Mission, Vadodara, Swami Nikhileshwaranand, is actively helping me. And I am also hopeful that the UP chief minister Akhilesh Yadav, who has already given me Rs 25 lakh for my Everest feat, will do his bit for the academy too. I am now invited to give lectures. I don't cook up anything. When I speak, I do so from the heart. With each passing day the academy fund and my confidence are growing. I am certain that I will raise the amount. If nothing works, I will even go from door to door to seek funds, accepting as little as Re 1. Anything is possible once we set our minds to it. I've done this once before. I am ready to do it again.

ACKNOWLEDGEMENTS

I AM THE SUM TOTAL OF THE KINDNESS AND LOVE bestowed on me by countless people. Were it not for them, I would not be here today. In fact this book would not have become a reality either.

Recounting everybody's contribution is difficult and I know that I am going to miss some people out. So, before I start, I want to apologize to anyone I might have forgotten to mention here.

I begin by recalling the contribution of my immediate family – my father, late army man Harendra Kumar Sinha, who pumped up enough confidence and determination in me since my childhood days. My mother Gyan Bala Sinha, sister Laxmi, brother Rahul, brother-in-law Om Prakash, my nephew Raja as well as my cousin Satyendra Sinha. Had it not been for these members of my family, who stood behind me like a rock, I wouldn't have been here.

Now, let me bring in my extended family.

I must recall the contribution of people like Pintu Kashyap – the man who spotted me lying by the railway track. Had he not brought helping hands with him, I would have died a very lonely and painful death.

I can't ever forget B.C. Yadav, the pharmacist at the Bareilly district hospital who donated blood to save my life.

My Everest feat wouldn't have been possible without the two wonderful brothers – Shailesh and Rakesh Srivastava – who donated the artificial limb, which I used to climb the Everest and a couple of other peaks too. The limb is still in great shape!

To the wonderful doctors at AIIMS who treated me, Dr Vijay Sharma, Dr Sushma, Dr M.C. Mishra, Dr V. Katiyar, thank you.

Thanks to Hanmantrao Gaikwad, the chairman and managing director of BVG India Ltd, and Sanjay bhai.

Bachendri Pal ma'am and Rajendra Palji – the contribution of the Pals to my life is huge. They have always played the role of friend, philosopher and guide.

Thanks to Prateek Bhowmick, my chief training

instructor along with Bachendri Pal ma'am's brother.

I can't miss out P.P. Kapadia, the group manager of the Tata Steel Adventure Foundation, for taking care of us, and Sanjeev Paul, the vice president of Tata Steel, who flagged me off on my Everest trip.

Thanks to Shahnaz Hussain for giving me beauty tips and training on my AIIMS hospital bed.

Also thanks to Nirmal Jeet Singh Kalsi, joint secretary in the union home ministry, for encouraging me and for going out of his way to check if I could get a job.

Thanks to Ramakrishna Mission for supporting me on my Everest mission.

I was extremely lucky to have met some very helpful politicians. Prime Minister Narendra Modi deserves a special mention – as the then chief minister of Gujarat he first tweeted my Everest triumph and then honoured me in Gujarat for the feat and promised help for my academy dream too. Thanks Modiji. The then BJP chief (and now union home minister) Rajnath Singh had suggested that if I wanted to take up shooting as a career he could help through Jaspal Rana, who is a prominent shooter and his relative. Thanks Rajnathji, you have been very helpful. I wish to acknowledge the contribution of Congress chief Sonia Gandhi who rushed the very helpful Ajay Maken to meet me at the trauma centre in Lucknow. Maken really impressed me with his quiet efficiency. I wish to record my heartfelt gratitude to UP chief minister Akhilesh Yadav for being so refreshingly different. I remember the then BSP minister Ram Achal Rajbhar simply because he was among the first few politicians to realize that the family of a poor girl who is battling for survival needs more than lip sympathy. I also wish to thank Lucknow BJP leader Neeraj Saxena who organized a candlelight march to gather support for me when I really needed it.

Manish Chandra Pandey's contribution is immense. Without him, this book may not have happened. The story is mine but it is he who gave a meaningful shape to my triumph with his wordplay, which has heightened the book's appeal enormously.

A special word of thanks to my publisher, Chiki Sarkar. Thanks, Chiki, for providing this platform. I hope our association continues.

I must also mention Ratika Bhargava, the deputy chief copy editor at *Hindustan Times*, who played a wonderful host and prepared delectable dishes besides making helpful suggestions when this book was being written.

And last but not the least, let me acknowledge the contribution of two wonderful cricketers with big hearts – Yuvraj Singh and Harbhajan Singh. As soon as they heard about my tragedy they sent monetary help. Perhaps it is because of the good wishes Yuvraj has accumulated over the years that he triumphed over cancer too. Thanks Yuvi, thanks Bhajji!

making helpful suggestions when this book was being written.

And last but not the least, let me acknowledge the contribution of two wonderful cricketers who are my friends—Yuvraj Singh and Harbhajan Singh. As soon as they heard about my malady they sent monetary help. Perhaps it is because of the good wishes Yuvraj has accumulated over the years that he triumphed over cancer too. Thanks Yuvi, thanks Bhajji!